# BEYOND THE BRONX

## FROM PRISON TO PURPOSE

## SEAN MARTIN

REAL SUCCESS MENTORS LLC

# CONTENTS

Acknowledgements     1

Introduction     3

1. Beyond the Bronx     28

2. All Success Begins with Belief     42

Fullpage image     57

3. Writing It Down Habits and Goals     58

4. Life is A Game. Learn How to Play It.     74

5. Relationship Capital     102

6. Eliminate Blame and Take Back Your Power     118

7. Health is Wealth     136

8.  Energy                                        164

9.  Love and Gratitude—The Heart of        188
    Purpose

Conclusion                                     203

Chapter                                        215

About the Author                               216

# ACKNOWLEDGEMENTS

Before anything else, I want to thank the Source—God, the all-knowing vibration that moves through everything, whether we see it or not. The truth is, none of us know how all this works. But somewhere between faith and proof, in that space where we choose to believe, that's where the magic happens. That's where life starts to make sense.

I want to thank my wife, who saved me in my darkest hour, and my children Sophia and Lucas, who gave me true purpose for the first time in my life. To my mother, my greatest teacher, who early on planted the seed that the glass was indeed half full.

To Tony Robbins—I first picked up *Awaken the Giant Within* while in prison thirteen years before I met you in person and shared that story with you in Maui. That full-circle moment was the validation I was badly needing from a father figure I never had. To Dean Graziosi and my Zenith Family who've shown me what life can look like when you design it around family and Impact.

And to James Hallman of WriteWorks who helped me write this book and give it a voice that I could be proud of.

# INTRODUCTION

## Learning What You're Made Of

You learn things about yourself when you lose your freedom. When your hand is broken, and you're stuck behind a steel door with nothing but your own thoughts. That's what "the box" is like—solitary confinement. A dingy 8-foot x 10-foot cell with a barred window, metal platform bed with a dirty mattress built into the wall, a tiny stainless steel sink and matching toilet. Not exactly The Ritz Carlton, or even a Super 8 hotel for that matter. No letters, no commissary, and no contact except the occasional guard sliding a tray of food through a slot in the door. You don't get to shave. You stink, so you scrub your armpits in the sink a few times a day just to keep from gagging on yourself. The showers come twice a week in a four-by-four square stall covered in grime and hair and God knows what else. But you go, because it's what you can get and because you smell like a wet dog's ass.

Whatever's on the tray is what you eat. There's nothing else coming. If you're lucky, a book cart rolls by with a few paperbacks worth reading. And you didn't get to choose. Whatever three they slid through the door was what you were reading. So, what does one do with all this time you ask? Well, you might do push-ups, sit-ups, and pace the length of your cell. But I couldn't do any of that. My hand was wrecked from the fight that landed me in here. So, I just sat there alone with those random books and my thoughts. How the fuck did I end up here?

Long story short, I wound up here because someone had been stealing from my locker. Little things, mostly just commissary items, nothing serious, but enough to let me know I was being targeted by a sneak thief. And in prison, when someone comes after you, everyone's watching to see how you'll respond. Of course, I only had two months left on my bid. Two months...I could've just ridden it out. But I knew if I didn't act, I'd be marked a sucker, and I couldn't have that. First of all, because I'm not one, and more importantly, the other inmates would keep coming. That's how it works in prison. It's not about what you lose, it's about what you're willing to tolerate, and about how you stand your ground.

So one day, I made a choice. I laced up my Timberland boots, threw on my standard issue prison slacks and my work gloves (which we were allowed to use for working out), and I went into the day room ready to let this dude know that I wasn't to be fucked with. I assumed the guilty party was the same guy I'd had problems with in the past. We had shared some mutual associates, but we didn't like each other.

That day, I didn't ask questions. I didn't square up. I just walked in, kicked him to the floor and hammered on him until I saw red. That's how I messed up my hand: I broke it on the top of his head as I beat him unconscious; I beat him until he came to; then I beat him some more. One of the other guys I was cool with finally stepped in, and said, "Bro, I think he's had enough" putting his arm and shoulder in between me like a boxing referee when the bell rings at the end of a round. I was lost in a tornado of Anger; Fear and Rage; my blood pumping fast enough to fill an Olympic-sized swimming pool. But at that moment when the other guy interjected, I snapped out of it. The damage was done, and I'd made the point I set out to make. But I thank God for that man who stepped in because it could have ended far worse for myself and the guy, I hurt that day.

That fight changed everything. When I came back from the box, it was smooth sailing for the rest of my stay. Nobody gave me any problems again. Even guys who hadn't seen the fight firsthand had heard the story. One dude looked at me and said, "You didn't just fuck that guy up. You demolished him." And in prison, a reputation like that matters.

See, respect in prison doesn't come from how well you talk. It doesn't come from being polite, or smart, or good at staying out of trouble. It comes from violence; that's the currency. That's the language of being locked up. This was one lesson I learned from my co-defendant. "All motherfuckers in prison respect is violence." When I ran into them after my release from the box, he asked why I didn't just square up with the guy and "shoot the fair one," as they say. I told him the truth. Well, at least half of it. I wasn't trying to give the man a chance to hit me. I'd already made the decision to lay him out, and I wasn't taking chances. And what I didn't tell them was that I was afraid. In my mind, the line had already been crossed. It wasn't about fairness anymore. This was about survival. About proving to everyone that I wasn't a sucker. That I wasn't going to let anyone fuck with me and get away with it. Of course, later I found out it wasn't even the guy I thought it was. Some other guy had been going through my stuff. One of the much scarier inmates; a real gorilla. The kind of man you don't want to go toe-to-toe with. And when I learned that, I remember thinking that I probably wouldn't have done anything had I known the truth. Prison, like any community, corporation or organization has a hierarchy. And the measure of progress was respect. Looking back now, I know that the only person I was trying to prove something to was me.

I got the facts wrong, but that didn't matter. What mattered is that I'd stood up for myself.

Now, I'm not proud of what I did. But I'm not ashamed either. At least not anymore. That part of me—the part that came out in that moment—it's still there. That killer instinct is alive and well. But I've learned a lot since then, and that part doesn't get to run the show. Not anymore. You see, though unconventional, my path has forced so many lessons on me. Prison was just one of many experiences that have shaped my life and my story. I mean, who do you know who goes to college, creates a somewhat successful career earning six figures and THEN goes to prison for two years? "Me, dat's who!" in my best Tony Montana from *Scarface* voice.

This is MY story and while I am a big dreamer, I don't think I could have imagined the life to follow. Since then, I've built successful businesses, made a lot of money, started a beautiful family, and have an incredible future ahead of me. I don't know how much of this would have happened if I didn't wind up in lockup for a couple years. And I have to acknowledge that something of my early years, all those struggles that came out of being a child of poverty and hardship did a lot to shape the way I learned to handle things. Maybe I went a little too far all those years ago, but I think part of my success has come from a willingness to push just a little harder than the other guy.

## The Honest Hustler

Before prison, I had what looked like a decent life. I was a medical marketing rep for a radiology facility. My job was to go around to doctors' offices, drop off donuts, smooth talk the staff, and make sure they were referring patients to our imaging centers. We called it the "donut boy" hustle, but it was legit. I was making sixty, maybe seventy grand a year, and I was good at it. I didn't have to report to an office and didn't punch a clock. I managed my own schedule, showed results, and got to live how I wanted.

But that paycheck? It was just enough to make ends meet. I was in my mid 20's and enjoying life. And living in NYC is expensive. Even in The Bronx. And yes, there are plenty of decent neighborhoods in my borough, for those who only associate it with the Yankees and crime. But that is neither here, nor there.

Around the same time, I started hustling knockoff clothes—fake Nike Jordans, Ed Hardy hats and t-shirts, Juicy Couture sweatsuits. All the stuff people wanted but couldn't afford. If you knew where to look—28th Street and Chinatown—the Nigerian vendors would sell in bulk and an enterprising person could flip it fast. I'd buy a pair of knockoff Jordans for $30, sell them for $60-$75. Same with the clothes. The markup was clean, the product looked good, and if you could manage your hustle, you could make a good bit of cash.

The first time I tried it, it was a few days before Christmas when people rush to do last minute shopping. I took $900 I had recruited my little brother (cheap labor) and drove down to NYC. We filled my trunk with gear, drove back up to The Bronx, and posted up in front of an Old Navy on White Plains Road all weekend right there on the sidewalk, illegally parked and all. Looking back, it all sounds ridiculous. But back then it was normal. And exciting as hell! By the end of the weekend, I'd turned that $900 into over four grand.

And that was it. I was in.

I kept my day job, but the side hustle grew fast. I was making more money selling the clothing than at my day job. Eventually I had shelves built in my house, like a little boutique. People I trusted would come to the shop: friends, neighbors, girls from the doctors' offices and their boyfriends and kids. People couldn't afford a $200 pair of sweatpants, but they'd happily pay $60 for something that looked just as good. And I never pretended my stuff was legit. If someone asked, "Are these authentic?" I'd say, "Come on. You're buying this out of the trunk of my car. But I'm giving you a fair deal." Some bought. Some declined. But no one could say they were ever misled, cheated, or hustled.

I liked to think of myself as an *honest hustler*. I wasn't out to scam people. Instead, I just gave my customers something they wanted at a price they could afford, and I told the truth about what it was. That was my code.

The hustle worked its way into everything. My day job gave me access to offices full of people who wanted what I had. My routes became supply runs. My business card could get me past any front desk. I was making two or three grand a week on top of my salary, working when I wanted, doing things on my own terms. That lifestyle—the freedom, money, and respect—it gets addictive. You start to feel invincible. And when the money comes easy, you blow it just as easy and you start looking for more.

So, I did. And my operation expanded into more frowned upon activity. I had a friend moving volumes of MDMA, back then known as Ecstasy. He didn't always have the ability to run around all weekend, so occasionally I stepped in. I moved his product, made cash, and kept a low profile. I even set the record one weekend for most pills sold in a day. In retrospect, I don't know that I should have been quite as proud of that as I was, but that's how your value system starts to get twisted up. You start measuring yourself in sales, in clout, and who knows your name at the club.

You can imagine that we partied hard. I was using too—ecstasy was my drug of choice at the time. My car was my office. My trunk; the stockroom. I had money in my pocket, and a new fit every

Friday and Saturday night. I thought I had the game figured out.

The reckoning came on one of those nights I shouldn't have been out, in a place I shouldn't have been. I was with my friend at a seedy bar in one of the sketchier parts of The Bronx. The crowd wasn't working class or even the hustlers with class, but the lowest level operators on the streets: the addicted, the desperate, and the predatory. I walked into their world like a peacock—fresh butter-soft leather jacket and a flashy watch; all eyes were on me. I stood out, and not in a good way. Truth be told it wasn't my scene. It wasn't a place I would ever hang out in, but that night I was tagging along with a friend.

By the end of the night, I'd managed to attract the wrong kind of attention. A crew of stick-up kids at the bar decided that I'd be an easy mark. But it didn't play out like that. When they came after us, we fought back. Violence ensued. Weapons were used. And when the dust settled, we'd stopped being the victims—we turned the tables and were after them.

It's still hard to talk about what happened that night. Not because I'm hiding anything, but because the story is messy. The stick-up crew turned out to be part of an interstate trafficking ring and were already targets of law enforcement. They had a lot more to lose, so when the authorities got involved, they tried to rewrite the story of what happened that night to make me look like the instigator.

The fabrications didn't really help them much. They were wanted on a range of charges already, so by the time I was copping to my own sentence, unbeknownst to me, they were already in jail. But their bullshit had wound up getting us caught up already. The prosecutor literally tried to throw the book at us. I still remember when the prosecutors presented the charges to me. I was stunned.

Eventually, I pled out. I was charged with attempted robbery in the second degree, an E-class felony. I'd have to spend two years in prison and would receive two years post-release supervision. But that moment—the crime, the setup, the experience of the courtroom—was the first crack in my worldview. I was learning that I wasn't a gangster; I wasn't some street legend. I was a man who thought he could ride the line between legit and illegal, and got stuck on the wrong side. The streets don't respect halfway crooks.

And that's how I ended up doing time. Not because I was the worst guy in the room, but because I'd let my pride run the show. And I put myself in the wrong places and around the wrong people, chasing money, clout, and a good time.

## Violence

Prison doesn't just confine you. It reprograms the way you understand the world. It teaches you new rules; brutal, simple rules—that you either learn fast or get swallowed by.

One of the first things you figure out is that prison has its own economy. Not just built on stamps, or snacks, or favors, but built on *respect*. And the currency of respect, more than anything else, is violence.

I saw that early on, even before I got to the main facility. Whether it was at Rikers Island or upstate, it was always the same: how a man carried himself mattered less than what he was willing to do if pushed. People in prison didn't care that much about your past. Instead, they watched how you moved in the present. Whether you looked people in the eye. Whether you stood your ground. Whether you flinched when threatened. They were literally and figuratively sizing you up all the time.

I was never a gangster, and I had a way of speaking that was clear, confident, and educated. It made people pay attention. It also made some of them uncomfortable. The counselors noticed and probably treated me better as a result. But the inmates noticed too. For some, this made me a leader. For others it made me a target. In prison, those can be the same thing. Being conspicuous can often work against you.

In my case, I was eventually asked to take a position as the inmate liaison for the counseling program. It was an unofficial role, but everyone knew what it meant: I had the counselors' ears. I could speak for the population in meetings, smooth out tensions between the institution and the inmates, and pass along their concerns. Being assigned to serve as their liaison left me holding space in a community that I didn't really belong with. It made me feel isolated in a whole new way.

But there were some perks that came along with it. I got my own room. No bunks—just a door. Sounds like a luxury, and in some ways, it was. But it also makes you more visible. People started watching me more closely. Some respected the work I was doing; others resented it.

See, if I hadn't had a private room, I probably wouldn't have been robbed. That's what eventually led to the fight—the one that put me in the box.

Prison is different from the street. On the streets, you can bullshit your way out of most situations. You can flex with your mouth, or your car, or your clothes. Inside? None of that matters. The ease you "move" with matters. Your fists matter. Your silence matters. Your tolerance matters. And when that tolerance runs out, everyone watches what you do next. Because one thing's for sure: at some point someone WILL test you, and how you react will determine how comfortable or uncomfortable the rest of your stay will be. Just because you run a good hustle out there, doesn't mean you can expect the same success or respect inside.

People assume that prison is full of hardened criminals. And yes, there are some. But there are also regular men in hard situations. Men who'd been broken before they got there. Men who spend their time scheming, lying, or looking for someone to stand behind. And if you're not careful, one of them might decide to take that inch you give and make it a mile.

I don't know if I took all the right lessons from my experience. But what I know is that the man I was when I walked into prison, the confident, charming, "honest hustler" Sean, couldn't survive there. Prison forced him to grow up and become someone I wouldn't fully understand until later.

That version of me—the one shaped by the pressure of fear and an overdeveloped need to prove myself—isn't the one writing this book.

## My Rite of Passage

For most of my life, I thought being a man meant standing your ground. Never backing down. Handling your business, no matter the cost. That mindset helped me survive—but it also nearly destroyed me.

It took me years of reflection and growth, not to mention a prison sentence, to realize I wasn't living as the man I wanted to be. I was living as the man I thought I had to be.

I didn't grow up with a father. And while my mom did everything she could, she couldn't teach me how to be a man. And because I didn't have that example, I started picking up my cues from the only men I had available to me as "role models." The cats from the streets. The "OG's"—which stands for Original Gangsters. Not all of them were gangsters though. Many of them were just older survivors of the same struggle who never made it out of the neighborhood. But we didn't know that at the time. So, we looked up to them. I also found my examples of masculinity from movies we watched and the music we listened to: narratives about tough guys and hustlers; role models who equated manhood with aggression and dominance.

I wasn't a violent person by nature. But I believed, deep down, that if I let someone take advantage of me—even once—it meant I didn't count. That if I was weak, I deserved whatever came next. And that belief got me locked up. That belief got me to take a savage anger out on a man who'd, in truth, done me no wrong. It was more than pride: it was about fear. Not fear of him, but fear of who I'd be turned into if I didn't respond. I was terrified of not being seen as a man.

But here's what I finally had to face: If your worth depends on what other people think of you, you're not free. And if your idea of strength is based on how dangerous you seem, you're already trapped.

That realization hit me hard, and once I saw that clearly, I couldn't go back. That's when I started to build something new for myself. Not just a new reputation, but a new foundation.

I didn't want to live by the old rules anymore. I didn't want to be feared—I wanted to be respected. I wanted to be trusted. I wanted to be the kind of man who didn't have to raise his voice or his fists to be heard. I wanted to be the kind of man who knew exactly who he was and didn't need to prove it every time he walked into a room.

Which brings me to what this book is for. I'd like it to be a tool for people who've been stuck in cycles that don't serve them anymore but aren't sure how to step out. For people who want to escape the belief that where we come from decides where we can go.

If there's one truth I've earned, it's this: you are stronger than you think. But strength isn't about how hard you hit. It's about how well you know yourself—and what you do with that knowledge. Strength comes from knowing when to stand tall and when to walk away and from understanding that your past doesn't define your future. You can take ownership of your choices—not with guilt, but with clarity.

I might have had to learn a lot of that the hard way, but my hope is that you don't have to.

## Looking Forward

I didn't write this book to brag, or to scare you straight, or to dwell on my past. I wrote it because I want you to know that whatever you've been through, however bad it's gotten—there's still a way forward. And it starts with choosing to believe that you get to write your own story. It's about what happens when you stop letting your past define you and start building the future you actually want.

After all, you don't have to go to prison to feel trapped; you don't need a rap sheet to carry shame. And you don't need to hit rock bottom to decide *I want more than this.*

It's divided into chapters that cover what I believe are the core elements of lasting success—not just in terms of money or titles, but in terms of who you are and how you show up in the world. Things like:

- Believing in yourself, even when it feels impossible.

- Turning adversity into a source of power.

- Building habits that serve your vision.

- Learning to love yourself—and others—fully.

- Forgiving your past and stepping into your purpose.

- Taking care of your body, mind, and spirit.

- Learning how to be in relationships that lift you up.

- And most importantly, never letting fear or shame rob you of your strength again.

I'll also try and offer you tools—things you can read, watch, or try—that helped me.

I won't pretend it's easy. Growth isn't comfortable. But if you've ever felt like the world wrote you off, or like you wrote yourself off, then this book is here to say: it's not too late. You can still write a better story.

I've lived both sides of the equation. I've been lost, I've been broken, and I've come out the other side with scars. But I also found a sense of purpose I didn't have as a younger man. If my story can serve to teach that change is possible, then I've done my job.

# 1

# BEYOND THE BRONX

## Where It All Started

Getting to where we want to be in life is a process. And whatever your journey, whatever road you find yourself following, and whatever opportunities that you find, we all start somewhere.

So where did I come from?

I was born in 1978, in the middle of a financial downturn that would shape the future of New York City and the people within it. I grew up in the Parkside Projects in The Bronx, which in the 1980s was a place in transition. You might even call it a community in foreclosure—disenfranchised, struggling, yet ever reshaping itself.

On any given summer day in the "bricks" (The Projects or PJS) back then, your whole block was alive, whether you wanted it to be or not. The park was full of life and action. Sneakers squeaking up and down as the guys ran full court games of basketball on one of our neighborhoods two courts. The hierarchy stated that the one closest to the benches was reserved for the big boys and the other for everyone else. Loud Hip-Hop music would often blast from the row of benches where at least two more teams were waiting on "next" (their turn to play). Our park also had handball courts. Four of them. That's where the Puerto Ricans and Latinos tended to gather. And you often heard the competing sounds of salsa and freestyle music banging from equally capable 1990s style D battery powered boomboxes.

New York City is indeed one of the most diverse places on the planet. However, it is also one of the most segregated. Many neighborhoods consist largely of concentrations of people from one particular part of the world who came here as immigrants. They came over and gradually helped each other succeed and improve the quality of life, not only for individuals but for the community as a whole. They'd start businesses, open places of worship, and create almost self-sustaining economies within their own neighborhoods. As a result, quite a few neighborhoods completely shifted in just a generation. This is the immigrant story of NYC, and it is beautiful.

But there is a dynamic that I feel is a uniquely NYC thing: the relationship between African Americans and Latinos, particularly those from Puerto Rico. Blacks and Puerto Ricans have shared the burden of extreme and consistent poverty for generations in the City that Never Sleeps. During the Civil Rights days and into the 1970s, Blacks and Puerto Ricans struggled and fought hand in hand against systems designed to hold them back and keep them isolated. First, they struggled against poverty and discrimination;

then against heroin and Reagan era social service cuts; followed almost immediately by crack cocaine and the infamous Rockefeller Drug Laws which stole another generation of hope from our communities.

And for generation after generation, it could feel like the same story was being told over and over again. I know all too well that it can feel like there is very little hope. The unfortunate reality is that the only way up is often to get out completely. And when you *do* make it out, you usually don't look back. Unlike immigrant populations that come over here full of hope and bring a work ethic that lifts their entire community out of poverty, we remain stuck. Why is that? I believe many of us have been beaten into submission. Generations past were forced to stay down or get squashed. And so, many of us have given up and have accepted the culture of blame that comes from intergenerational trauma and frustration. I get it. Because that is where I come from.

I was raised on hip-hop, freestyle music, crack cocaine, and chaos. My story is uniquely New York,
something those from there will instantly understand. For others, I will try to paint a picture as
clearly as I can in the hopes of making my experience more relatable. This is a story of overcoming
adversity and claiming the life I always dreamt of.
Because it's not how you start in life, but how you
finish that ultimately defines you.

Growing up where I did, you learned early to keep
your head on a swivel. Every hallway smelled like
piss and weed, and every graffiti covered stairwell
could hide somebody you didn't want to meet.
Crack was just starting to tear through the neighborhood, and you could watch as it hollowed out
people you'd known your whole life. But there was
also resilience—kids playing in the street, grandmothers on benches or peaking from their win-
dows, watching everything like hawks, and neighbors who'd give you a plate of food even if they
didn't have much themselves. That's what it was:
beauty and struggle living shoulder to shoulder,

and you had to decide every day which of those you were going to carry with you.

In The Bronx of the '80s and early '90s, decay wasn't a metaphor. The sound of sirens was constant, but so was the sound of kids playing ball in the street. It wasn't all bleak—people built rich lives from the asphalt. But the city and the nation had turned its back on communities like mine, and everyone knew it. And unfortunately, this was nothing new.

So, I suppose that the more complex answer is that I come from poverty and struggle. And it taught me how to survive.

But more importantly than any of that, I come from LOVE. I had the love of my mother, who was an immigrant who came to the U.S. with her family at the age of eleven. She had me at 24 years old.

By the time we settled into Parkside Projects, the neighborhood was starting to slide. The previous inhabitants—mostly Jewish and Italian immigrants, many of them second-generation—had already moved out. And the few that were left and could afford to leave, began their exodus. There were holdouts, but they didn't last long as poverty deepened and crime increased. Change is always challenging under the best of circumstances, then came the drug epidemic. Crack cocaine started to flood the inner cities in the '80s, changing the neighborhood practically overnight. The streets descended into lawlessness. Young men were pulled (and sometimes pushed) into the drug trade, chasing the illusion of fast money and easy status. The increasingly brutal sentencing guidelines meant that families were fractured as fathers and brothers were getting "football numbers," The term that came to describe the sharp rise in double digit year prison sentences that offenders were given. The Rockefeller Drug Laws, put into effect in 1973 by mayor Nelson Rockerfeller, set extreme penalties for relatively low-level offenses. Selling or possessing drugs could land you between 15 and 25 years in prison, which meant that many young men and fathers were locked up for significant portions of their lives. This left way too many mothers, aunts, and grandmothers to hold things together as best they could at home.

When I was very young and we first moved into the Projects, I remember that our community had felt safe. All that started changing almost overnight. Our sense of security was steadily eroded and, ultimately, all but erased by the beginning of the 1990s.

But I had a shelter against this storm: my mother. The love I received at home from her outshined any of the violence happening outside our door. She was also educated. She finished high school and went on to earn degrees from Bronx Community College and City University of New York. The first and only one in her family to get a degree until our generation. She gave me a place of safety and stability, even as she struggled with her own demons. This was the 1980s after all. She had her own challenges in that environment—its drugs and nightlife got a hold of her too.

Regardless of her private struggles, she instilled the best in me: resilience, independence, and the belief that I was in control of my own destiny. Because she worked, I learned early on how to take care of myself. I was what they called a latchkey kid back then. By the age of eight, I was walking myself to school, coming home alone, completing my homework, and handling chores. I had to be self-sufficient. Today, I see how much of the world wants to shelter children against adversity, but for me, adversity would prove to be my training ground. I learned to keep my guard up, to protect myself, to read a room, and to recognize danger. Those lessons taught me more than any book ever could.

## The Power of Community

Despite the chaos, growing up in the projects wasn't all bad. There was community. We had playgrounds and basketball courts; we had games of manhunt (a version of "tag") that stretched across entire blocks. And there was an unspoken code: people looked out for each other. Even if you were a criminal, you knew that you had to look after your own and for your part of the neighborhood. For many, dealing drugs wasn't about ambition, it was about survival. It wasn't a glorified profession—it was a means to an end; a source of income in what was otherwise a desert of opportunity. And for me, I had to decide whether I would make my money through those means or find my own.

Fortunately, my mother also stressed the importance of education. She'd set the standard early. She learned English, graduated high school on time, and went on to complete college through the City University of New York system. I had always been expected to follow suit. That said, school was never my first love. I was more interested in the social scene outside of class. I excelled at making people laugh, and of course in pushing the boundaries. In other words, I often played the class clown. A talker and a bit disruptive. Not because I wasn't capable, but because I was bored.

The schoolwork came easily to me, and I wasn't being challenged in the ways I needed.

Music was also an essential outlet for young me, I started playing the saxophone as a kid, and it offered escape, structure, and deterrence. It kept me occupied on weekends when others were out in the street, getting into trouble and making poor choices. I spent hours in practice, honing my craft instead of testing the limits of the law. And I credit music, along with my mother's influence, for helping me break the cycles that trapped so many of the friends I grew up with.

## A Seed Was Planted

The truth is that poverty isn't just about lacking money or resources. It's a mindset. It's a lack of belief, a feeling of inevitability that keeps people stuck where they are. I saw it first hand—generations caught in the welfare system, not because they wanted to be, but because they didn't see a way out. That said, when my mother had my younger brother, she went on welfare for a time, and in some ways, we were better off than when she was working. The system was flawed, but it inadvertently revealed something to me: financial security isn't just about having money. It's about knowing how to navigate opportunities and make them work for you.

By the time I was a teenager, I had a choice to make. I had spent time on the periphery of street life, standing next to the guys who had the flashy clothes, the money, and the girls. But I also saw behind the curtain. Many of them were still living with their mothers and grandmothers, with nothing to their names but the cash in their pockets and a fancy pair of shoes. I didn't realize at the time, but all the lifestyle was just smoke and mirrors.

And so, I had to decide: was I going to be the product of my environment, or was I going to take control of my future?

I was lucky. My mother's lessons stuck. She had always told me, *If you think you can, you can. If you*

*think you can't, you can't. Either way, you're right.*
That belief carried me through. It drove me to find solutions instead of excuses. It helped me navigate moments of doubt and keep one foot firmly on the path forward, even when I was tempted to stray.

I won't say I was perfect. I made mistakes. I tested limits. I walked a fine line between the streets and a better future. I hung out with drug dealers at parties, young and naive enough to think they were cool. I got into fights. I took some beatings and gave some back. But that's not to say I didn't have to stumble to understand this. Street thinking managed to get a strong hold on me for a time and would eventually catch up to me. But the truth is that I was never a tough guy; I never fully committed to "the life." And because of that, I never fell so far that I couldn't come back.

The upshot is that our environment tells us something of who we are and who we can become. It can whisper limitations into our ears and set invisible boundaries around what we believe we're capable of. The streets of the Bronx whispered to me. They taught me that there's a pecking order out there, one that I was never going to be at the top of. There was a limit to how far I'd ever be able to go as long as I didn't look beyond them. And for that, I'm grateful to my mother. She threw a wrench into that system. She broke the cycle for me before I even knew what the cycle was. She planted a seed in me that told me I could be more. That I could define my own future.

And that lesson changed everything.

Because where you come from matters—but it doesn't define where you have to go.

# 2

# ALL SUCCESS BEGINS WITH BELIEF

## Defining Success

What are we talking about when we talk about belief? Do you believe that you can be successful? Belief is what your mind accepts as true. Faith is what your heart holds onto, even when there's uncertainty. Faith will keep you going. But only belief will get you there.

That was always the question on my mind, but I didn't know what success looked like. Growing up, the closest examples I really saw were petty drug dealers with a few bucks in their pocket. And these guys always ended up falling on their face. Most of them would wind up in prison or worse. Hardly shining examples of how to get ahead.

So, what is success? What does it look like? My mother had a 4-year college education, but she never made more than $50,000 a year. When you're trying to support a household on that kind of income, money will always be tight. So, I knew that money was the way out: money was always a solution. But how the hell was I going to make enough money to change my life?

Fortunately, as a working mom, she made sure that we always had enough even when we didn't have enough. We had a relationship with the bodega (neighborhood grocery store), for example. They gave my mother a line of credit to help cover us when we didn't have enough money during that week before the paycheck came in. We were always good for it. But this taught me something about the importance of relationships: honoring your word and paying your debts. It also helped me understand that being responsible to the people in my life and my community was an important part of keeping control of my own life. These things would be imperative for my future.

Belief doesn't just come from yourself. It comes from the people in your life. My mother obviously believed in me, but I also got a lot of encouragement from my teachers. Sure, I had a few that couldn't see past my clowning around, but most of them realized that I had something special. They pushed me into the advanced classes, raising the bar for me and providing a higher set of expectations for myself. Thinking back, these were formative times, where I really started to see myself capable of accomplishing things that I could be proud of.

## No Male Role Models

But seeing something in yourself is harder when you don't have a male role model in your life. Negative self-talk can be overwhelming when you're overweight and struggle with acne. When I was growing up, I had to struggle with these things. None of the men in my mother's life were really "father figures," and she wasn't really looking to bring them in for that purpose anyways. She chose them for companionship and security, but not to raise her kids.

Moreover, I was a pretty awkward kid, heavyset with bad skin. I didn't have a lot of confidence, and my self-esteem took regular hits. Kids are mean enough, but maybe poverty and instability makes them worse. I can't even imagine what that looks like now with social media where you're only seeing the highlight reels of people's lives. Worse to think everything is filtered, setting up impossible expectations for young people.

There were no filters back in our day. You were either cool, or you weren't. You couldn't fake it online. I wasn't the coolest and neither was my clique. But we weren't the geekiest either. We were somewhere in the middle of the pecking order. This meant that we might get pushed around, but we got to do some pushing of our own. Mind you,

I'm not condoning this, I'm just saying that there was a hierarchy and I was consigned to my place in it.

## Time to Grow Up, Mama's Boy

Like most of us, I definitely struggled during my teenage years. But I had a few things going for me.

I think it helped that I worked. From the age of twelve on, I would always have a part-time job of some type, especially during the summers. Working instilled a sense of responsibility, a work ethic, and a knowledge of money and how far it could go. More importantly, working put the dramas of high school into perspective and helped me understand that there were more important things. I really think every young person should get work experience. The lessons you learn from earning your own money are invaluable (something important for parents to remember—especially if they actually have means).

Another big event in my life was becoming a big brother at age 13. Until then, I was an only child—the recipient of all my mother's love and attention. Looking back now, I can say that this is when the streets and all their trappings started to influence my behavior more and more. I began looking to the neighborhood for whatever attention I was not getting at home.

Getting into sports changed things for me as well. I'd had a short stint in little league when I was a kid, but I didn't get to stick with it. The summer following my junior year though, I wasn't working and decided to pick up basketball. I might have been overweight, but I also had height, which meant I had some natural talent. After playing basketball for countless hours a day for an entire summer, I found myself back for my senior year of high school, weighing considerably less and finally coming into my good looks and charm (although the acne was still a killer).

Even better, now girls started paying attention to me. For guys in high school, girls were always a measuring stick for how cool and attractive you were. Their attention also said something about how good you could feel about yourself. So, my senior year was good. I was hanging out with the cooler kids, and I was rising in the ranks of social importantness (if that's even a word). I attended La Guardia High School of Music and Art and was surrounded by talent. Some of the young musicians I went to school with were literally world class.

But I didn't really apply myself during my senior year. The kids that were the best worked the hardest—they weren't just the most talented. So, while I had talent and some work ethic, I came to recognize that I wasn't putting in the work that was needed to get to the top. I was kind of wavering, didn't know what I wanted to do with myself, and spent my last year just kinda hanging out. I'd become a bare minimum kind of guy, coasting through high school on my natural talent and my smarts.

I actually missed one class 40 times but still managed to pass: a testament to my half-assed approach to life that year. I started drinking and was hanging out in the streets a lot more, which would also have consequences at school. But I still always kept a job because I had become accustomed to making my own money.

There were a couple of factors that allowed me to stray in my formative teenage years. I think that not having a father figure or male role model made it tougher for me, for one. I didn't have anyone to lean on. I didn't have anyone to bounce things off—just my mom or other friends. I had good teachers, but none of them necessarily took me under their wing. I never had one of those movie moments where some magical figure swooped in and changed the trajectory of my life. No big epiphany of who I wanted to be and how I wanted to get there. So this was a period in my life where I didn't necessarily believe in myself. I was just kind of going through the motions: work, school, hang out, repeat.

All that changed in community college, which I only signed up for because I was too lazy to take the entrance exams for a four-year school. Not that there was anything wrong with that. My mother went to Bronx Community College herself, so in some ways, I was just following in her footsteps but not exactly making generational progress. Fortunately, God's got a plan for us all, and mine seemed to start at Bronx Community College a generation after my mother had graduated. And it was actually an awesome experience. Admittedly, my first year there was humdrum. I still worked after school, took the bus, rode the train and lived the traditional city life. I was putting in work though, building the character traits that would turn me into a young man.

By the time I started down that road, I'd already learned to do my own thing. My mother was busy raising my siblings who were 13 and 16 years my junior. I was the oldest; the more mature one and was slowly learning to steer my own course. Community College was an essential step.

By my second year of community college, I really began to blossom into the leader that I was meant to be. I took on a leadership role on campus, becoming the president of the honor society. I was a natural people person and a promoter extraordinaire. I worked at campus like it was my canvas, promoting all types of organizations and events for myself and my fellow students. I graduated with honors, which helped me to recover from my slack performance during my senior year of high school. I earned scholarships and grants that enabled me to attend Ithaca College, a private four-year institution in upstate New York.

At Ithaca, I continued to excel socially, but still wasn't the best student. There was definitely a pattern here. I was just finding too much distraction. And looking back now, I think I probably had ADHD. It didn't matter though; at Ithaca, I was starting to believe again. I was starting to believe in my abilities. I was starting to take chances on myself. I was starting to make something out of nothing. I was turning my ideas into motion, and

I was turning my growing inertia into successes. I DJed for the school's radio station, promoted parties, started grassroots marketing companies for local businesses, and ran advertising campaigns for other organizations.

At one point, I canvassed an entire small town with our flyers for events, bus stop to bus stop and door to door. I was putting in the work, but I was doing it for myself. I learned that if I wanted to do something, I would do it my way and I was going to go at it hard. This confidence could be a bit of a double-edged sword, but my belief in myself became stronger; indomitable. I learned that I was worth taking a chance on, but I just didn't fit into groups. I was a loner. Nor was I the typical leadership type, but I wasn't a follower either. I marched to the beat of my own drum. I tried things that other people were afraid to try.

## Get a Different Perspective

Our journey into success begins by developing a belief in ourselves. But there are a few things I wish I had better understood early on in my journey.

I wish I had known about therapy earlier, but that wasn't part of my world. Where I came from, you didn't talk to anyone about your problems. You figured them out on your own. You pushed through by pushing them down. But muscling through your problems doesn't make them disappear—it just makes them heavier. Therapy later in life helped me see the things I had buried. It helped me understand why I always felt like I had to prove something, why I couldn't shake certain doubts, and why I kept hitting the same walls over and over.

These days, I'm a big proponent of people seeking out help through therapy. I think they need to develop their emotional intelligence and to find a deeper understanding of themselves, the things they've been through, and how those experiences impact their lives. Only by facing these things can we get over the hump, instead of just ignoring our problems. Therapy offers a smoother road, but the stigma that keeps people out is real. Not to mention the challenge of finding services.

Therapy helps you understand that there's a gravity to your past. If you don't deal with it, it pulls you back—back into old habits, old mindsets, old identities. You keep living in the story of who you *were* instead of the story of who you *could be*. What I've learned is that identity isn't fixed; it's built on the stories we tell ourselves about what we've been through. And if you never stop to examine those stories, they start writing the script for your life. Therapy was one of the first tools to help me identify that cycle. It gave me space to look at where I'd come from without judgment—and the tools to separate what happened to me from who I am. That process didn't erase the past, but it changed my relationship to it. Instead of letting it define me, I started using it to understand myself, to make better choices, to shift. Not overnight. But slowly, I stopped reacting from old wounds and started responding with intention. I also can't quite shake the feeling that it would have been good if I'd had a male role model or a mentor to look up to and show me the ropes; to give me a blueprint of what a man looked like. I could have used some guidance around the conversations I was having in my own mind—the self-doubt and nagging questions around whether I was good enough. You know, all the things that I think young men struggle with on the road to maturity. Unfortunately, as a young person, I had to do without.

Nevertheless, somewhere along the way, I learned that betting on myself was worth it. I started seeing my ideas turn into action, my actions into results. Not always good results, but results nevertheless. From these, I learned that I wasn't just a passenger in my own life—I was the driver.

I was never the type to fit neatly into a box. I was a square peg in a world full of round holes. And that was okay. It meant I had to carve out my own space and blaze my own trail. It meant taking risks and making moves that didn't always make sense to others, but that felt right to me. And most importantly, it meant believing—really *believing*—that I was capable of more.

## In Summary:

- All success starts with belief—before money, before status, before anything else.

- Overcoming negative self-talk is crucial to breaking out of mediocrity.

- Work ethic and responsibility shape your future more than raw talent.

- Therapy and self-reflection help remove the past's grip and allow for growth.

- Betting on yourself is the key to stepping into your potential and creating real success.

# 3

# WRITING IT DOWN HABITS AND GOALS

## Struggle = Stronger

Adversity was a big part of my childhood. Independence meant figuring things out on my own, and that built the foundation for the man I would eventually become. I think adversity is a missing component of many children's lives today. Things are just way too easy, and if life is always easy, why would anyone ever need to rise to the occasion? When everything is handed to you on a silver platter, you never develop the grit you'll need when life gets tough.

I remember when applying for a job meant physically going door to door and asking if a business was hiring. You carried a folder full of resumes, wore a respectable shirt and tie, and hit the pavement. Now you can mass market your resume via no less than a dozen job platforms. Want food? Click a few buttons and it's at your door in 45 minutes or less. And people *still* find a reason to complain about a lack of opportunity. The truth is closer to the fact that there isn't a lack of hunger anymore. Life is super comfortable and convenient. Success is the exact opposite. It's uncomfortable and inconvenient.

It's no different than going to the gym. You lift weights to break down your muscles so they can rebuild stronger. Life's challenges work the same way. Most of the lessons that shaped me didn't come from classrooms or textbooks—they came from being thrown into the fire and forced to figure it out. My most difficult moments helped me build an uncommon resilience to adversity.

Now that I'm a parent, I see how important resilience really is. I wrestle with how to instill it in my own kids. My wife and I don't always see eye to eye on this. She wants to protect our kids from everything. She has the time and resources to do it, and I get it—that's instinctual, especially for a mother. But I worry too much protection could hurt them in the long run. It's important to not be so sheltered that you forget the value of shelter.

So, we wrestle with the balance: how do we give our kids the things we never had while also teaching them responsibility? How do we provide comfort without making them soft? Parents who grew up with challenges they needed to overcome them know this well. You want your kids to have better lives than you did, but not at the cost of being too soft and fragile.

The truth is that adversity prepares you for life. If you never experience struggle, you don't know how to respond when hardship eventually shows up. And it *will* show up. Life doesn't care about fairness. It will test you. And if you've never learned how to take a punch, you'll fold. That's why adversity isn't something to avoid, but rather is something to embrace.

*This chapter isn't just about reading my story. It's also about taking stock of your own. Habits and goals only become real when you put them into practice, and the best way to start is by slowing down and asking yourself some tough questions. As you go through this chapter, you'll find short reflection prompts. They're simple, but don't skim past them. Pause. Write something down. Treat them like checkpoints: moments to connect what you're reading to the life you're actually living.*

*Here's your first one:*

*Think back to a struggle you faced growing up.*

*What did it teach you about yourself?*

*How might that same lesson serve you today?*

# Habits and Goals: WHAT Do You Want to Accomplish?

Habits are powerful. They can be the best of servants or the worst of masters. Whether we realize it or not, the habits we form early in life determine our trajectory. Good habits make success easier. Bad habits create obstacles we'll be battling for years.

One of the most important habits I ever developed was to set goals for myself. At 20 years old, I started writing down my goals, dreams, and visions for the future. At the time, I didn't fully understand the power of it. Years later, when I got sober in 2022, I came across an old notebook from college. In it I had scribbled a single question:

*"What would my life look like if I quit drugs and alcohol completely?"*

Even then, I knew those things weren't serving me. I just didn't have the courage, wisdom, or support I needed to make the change. I kept these habits because I was stuck in old patterns. And most importantly I never took any real action to address those things. Instead, I spent the next two decades drinking, using, partying, chasing women, overeating, and being reckless. I don't regret those years, but looking back, I can see that the desire for something better was always there. I just wasn't in the right environment to nurture it. I've also come to believe without a shadow of a doubt that I needed to have those experiences for me to become the man I am today.

Anyways. The act of writing that question down planted a seed. It took twenty years to sprout, but it did. When I saw those words later, I realized something: everything the self-development books say about goal-setting is true. Writing things down matters.

Without a vision, you're just drifting. If you don't know where you're going, you'll end up on whatever path life puts in front of you. I often tell young people: imagine you're standing on a train platform at Times Square in New York City.

Trains pull in and out all the time. Do you just hop on the first one that arrives? Of course not—you wait for the one that takes you to your destination. But in life, most people just jump on the first train without ever asking where it's headed.

If you don't have a vision for your future, you'll wander aimlessly. That's why I encourage everyone—especially young people—to write down their goals. Not just the safe, reasonable ones. Write something so big it scares you. Dream without limits. That's where greatness lives. That's where fear lives, too. And most people let the fear win.

How about you? Take a moment to reflect:

*What habits are shaping your life right now?*

*Which ones are pushing you forward towards your goals, and which ones are holding you back?*

## Don't Look Around. Look Up.

Here's another truth: no one does it alone. Other people are our greatest resource, yet too often we try to do it all on our own, or we look for help in the wrong places.

Most of the time, your immediate circle isn't equipped to guide you to your highest potential. That's especially true if you came from humble beginnings or with a poverty mindset like I did. Families and friends mean well, but sometimes they try to keep you safe by discouraging you from even trying. Or worse, they don't want to see you rise because it forces them to face their own limitations. I think one of the biggest dream killers is sharing your goals, and dreams with people who are completely unqualified to help you. And unfortunately, the people who love the most are often the guiltiest of this.

If you want to be great, you need to seek out greatness. Surround yourself with people who are already where you want to be. They can help you avoid years of trial and error. They've read the books, made the mistakes and have real world knowledge that can point out the traps before you fall into them.

But this starts with clarity. You can't find the right mentors unless you've taken the time to define your goals. Write them down. Dream them up. Then look for the people who can help you get there.

When we start our journey, first we learn from teachers. After our teachers, we learn from do-ers. A book can give you knowledge. A classroom can give you theory. But only by doing the thing, and learning from people who've done it, will you reach your potential.

How do we seek these people out? Take a moment to consider:

*Who is already living the kind of life you want?*

*What's one step you could take to learn from them?*

## The Power of Writing It Down

Writing things down is no small practice. The written word has carried civilizations, preserved cultures, and shaped history. And when it comes to our own lives, writing plays the same role. It preserves our intentions and helps us carry them forward.

One of the most powerful tools I've ever used is journaling. Countless studies show its benefits: greater happiness, more self-awareness, better problem-solving skills, and deeper empathy. But you don't need science to prove it. If you've ever written down a thought and come back to it years later, you already know its power.

When I decided to get sober after I found those old notes I'd written as a young man. Seeing that my younger self already knew what I needed to do—and that I had planted that intention decades earlier—was mind-blowing. Writing it down had set something in motion.

Another example comes from when I was in prison. I filled black-and-white composition notebooks with reflections, lessons, and goals. I wrote out visions for one year, five years, even twenty years down the road. I dreamed without limits, because what did I have to lose?

And here's the wild part... so many of those things came true.

- I wrote that I would be HAPPILY married to Jen with kids. And I am.

- I wrote that I would get in shape and respect the man I saw in the mirror. And I have.

- I wrote that I would make life-changing money and break cycles of poverty in my family. And though I have, that goal has morphed into something far greater. I aim to be an example of what is possible for the people that come from where I did and don't have role models to emulate.

- I wrote that I would use my success to give back to my community. And today,

I mentor and share my story to do exactly that.

- I wrote that I would write a book one day, and here you are reading my words.

Not every goal was accomplished on my timeline, and not everything was smooth. But the act of writing my goals down made them real. It was like sending a signal to myself (and maybe even to the universe) that said, *"This is where I want to go."*

Break out your notebook again:

*Write down one goal that feels impossible right now. Don't censor yourself. Just put it on paper. What scares you about it?*

*What excites you about it?*

## Mapping the Future

Journaling isn't just about dreaming big—it's about tracking progress. When you write things down, you create a record. You can look back and see how far you've come. You can recognize patterns that repeat in your life. You can catch subtle habits that might be holding you back. You can also use journaling as an outlet for personal emotions and for some of the deeper work that you will have to commit to.

Most of the time, I didn't go back and study my notebooks line by line. Not everything I wrote down would mean much beyond the moment I'd written it down. Sometimes I would just use it to express feelings or frustrations, and I'd often forget what I'd written. But just putting it on paper mattered. Writing planted seeds in my mind. The act gave me direction, even if quietly in the background.

And that's the point: writing is both practical and spiritual. It helps you clarify what you want, track what you're doing, and declare to yourself—and maybe even to the universe—that your life has a destination.

Take a minute to consider your own life:

*Look back at something you wrote years ago; a note, journal entry, or even a social media post. What does it reveal about who you were then, and how far you've come?*

## In Summary

- Struggles and challenges shape us, just like lifting heavy weights strengthens our muscles. Adversity builds resilience.

- The habits we form set the trajectory of our lives. Good habits make success easier; bad habits hold us back.

- Writing down your goals and journaling about your life creates clarity, accountability, and momentum. It turns intention into action and dreams into reality.

- Writing it down is more than memory—it's manifestation. It's how we move from drifting to designing, from surviving to thriving.

- No one succeeds alone. Seek out mentors and communities that push you higher.

# 4

# LIFE IS A GAME. LEARN HOW TO PLAY IT.

## Just Get Started

Recently, I partnered up with a couple other entrepreneurs to launch a new venture having to do with commercial real estate insurance. It's a new industry for us and inspired a partner to describe the process as "building the plane while we were in the air." I immediately took to the expression: that's exactly what it feels like when you're starting a business before all the systems are in place. You've got the idea. Maybe you've got some of the people you need to get started, but the structure? The backend? The SOPs? None of that is secure yet, so you're just figuring things out as problems come up.

We started talking about it and pitching the concept to parties we thought might be interested. We started figuring out solutions as problems came up, because it's only when you take action that the real work begins. That's when you see what needs fixing, what needs building. And as long as you've got the end goal in mind, you'll figure out the rest. You have to.

I came across a quote the other day from Richard Branson. He said, "If someone offers you an amazing opportunity and you're not sure you can do it, say yes—then figure it out later." That's been my life, man. Most people get caught up waiting for the right time, the right plan, or the right sign. Meanwhile, life's already moving, and if you're not moving with it, you're falling behind.

I've been in this spot before. Back in college, I was on the radio during my senior year, running the radio station at Ithaca College. A few of us started promoting parties at the clubs in town, and our marketing model was blowing up. We had a reputation: we were the party guys. We could always bring in great crowds with great energy. But then something clicked, and we saw a bigger opportunity.

See, local restaurants couldn't advertise directly on campus. It was against the rules for them to drop off their flyers in the dorms. But we could because we were students. So we started offering flyer drops. Businesses would pay us to walk through dorms and slip them under doors. We didn't have any permits or permission. We just had hustle.

And it worked. So, we went back, built marketing tiers, established different pricing packages, and started thinking bigger. as our service grew in popularity with local food spots, they also wanted access to Cornell University which was nearby. And while we didn't go to Cornell and really had no access to their dorms, we pitched the business there too. And we had to back up our promise, so we canvased the campus ourselves, guerilla style. We also recruited Cornell students, gave them a small cut of our sales, and built the operation out from there.

That's the thing. If you've got a real idea and a little bit of audacity, you *don't* need to have it all figured out. You just need to move—the rest comes if you've got the will to act.

## Whose Rules?

People love to talk about success, but they rarely talk about what it *really* takes to get there. And here's the truth: if you want to do something big, you're going to have to bend the rules. Maybe even break them sometimes. Not because you're reckless or lawless, but because most of the rules we live under aren't designed to help you succeed. They're designed to keep power right where it is.

This is probably why most of the successful people I've met—and I've met a lot—didn't follow the rules to get to the top. They stepped around them, and sometimes they blew right through them. It's not like they were out there slinging dope or robbing banks, but they found ways to disrupt stagnant systems by doing things differently and by going places they were told not to go. And sometimes, yeah, they paid the price. But they often managed to change the game.

And if I'm being completely honest, I was young, hungry, and didn't give a fuck. I think that was a result of coming from The Bronx. The rules were different. It was by any means necessary. As far as my college marketing business was concerned, the only thing the prohibition against advertising protected was the college's cut. So, we ignored it. We had to accept that not every rule exists to keep you safe. Some exist just to maintain control, protect profits, and to keep you in your place.

Take the healthcare system and the limitations imposed on it by the FDA here in the USA. I've got serious neck injuries. Stem cell therapy could help. It's been studied for decades. But I can't get it because this therapy hasn't been approved in the states. Not because it's unsafe, but because it threatens existing models of treatment and is considered politically charged by sections of the political class. Restricting it also ensures American pharmaceutical and insurance companies make billions more off pills and procedures. If they really cared about health, we'd have had access to stem cell treatments years ago. But these companies learned a long time ago that there's a lot more money to be made in keeping people sick.

Remember how many of our rules are established through lobbying. That's just legalized bribery, plain and simple. If you or I tried to pay someone not to testify in open court, or ignore critical research? We'd go to prison. But do it in the halls of government with a fancy title, it's business as usual. So again—whose rules are these?

Entrepreneurs break rules because they *have to*. Uber did. Airbnb did. They saw outdated systems and said, "Let's do this differently." And yeah, they pissed people off. They wrecked taxi medallion monopolies and rattled hotel chains in major cities across the world. But the system they disrupted wasn't fair to begin with.

That said—rule breaking isn't an excuse to be a piece of shit. There's a line, and that line matters.

There are rules worth breaking and there are rules that should *never* be touched. You don't harm people. You don't lie, cheat, or steal for your own gain. You don't take what isn't yours and call it innovation. That's not disruption—that's just being a parasite. The difference is intention. Are you breaking something that needs to be broken? Or are you just trying to get ahead at someone else's expense?

I think of it a bit like this. There are the laws of man, and there are laws of decency. The most basic of the latter is the golden rule: *Do unto others as you would have them do unto you.* It's the cleanest guide there is. If you wouldn't want someone else doing it to you, maybe don't do it to them—even if the law says you can. But if a rule is holding you back for no good reason? That's a boundary you can push.

The thing is that real success—real freedom—isn't for the obedient. It's for the ones willing to question the terms of the game. But grabbing that freedom comes with responsibility. You've got to have your own code, and you've got to be accountable to something deeper than the letter of the law.

So go ahead—challenge convention. Push boundaries. But be clear about what you're doing and why. The world doesn't need more winners. It needs people who win on *their own terms*—without losing (or stealing) souls.

**Change the world. Don't let it change you.**

That's the model I live by. I've met a lot of people in my life. Some of them pretend to be friends, some of them secretly root for me to fail. But I don't let that change how I treat people. I welcome them in; give them space to show me who they are. If someone burns me, I learn from it. But I don't close my heart. And that takes discipline; that takes integrity.

I wasn't always like this. I had to learn it the hard way.

I'm not trying to get philosophical or get too deep. I just know that at the end of the day, everything we believe—all our systems, all our institutions—they're just ways of thinking about relationships. They don't exist as immutable facts. There's no single truth about how to live, no perfect system that could manage the world. But you can make a lot of money while doing a lot of good. I've seen it done, and that's the mission I've set for myself.

Money isn't the root of all evil. It's the root of all *impact*. You want to have a bigger impact? You've got to be able to write bigger checks? And that means you need a bigger bank account. It might not sound fair, but that's the world we live in. It's the capitalist system America currently is. And for all the government spending, empty promises, and failed programs, some things are just stubbornly resistant to change. Poverty doesn't go away. Healthcare outcomes don't get all that much better. It seems the needle of desperation barely moves. So, I'm done waiting for other people to fix it. I'd rather play the game, win, and set myself up to be the change.

I used to be more idealistic. When I was younger, I was angry. After all, I came from nothing, growing up poor during the Reagan years. I saw firsthand how American capitalism left people behind, sometimes in the cruelest of ways.

Four decades later, we've got a president working from a familiar playbook. The difference is that I've gone from being the child of a working-poor single mom in the 1980s to standing among the 1% now.

People say, *"We've never been this divided."* Really? Ever heard of the Civil War? How about the turmoil of the 1960s? Rodney King, O.J. Simpson, immigration battles, voter suppression—the story of America has always included conflict and fracture. Division isn't new. What is new is the 24-hour access to media coverage that amplifies people's biases and fears using an algorithm that keeps them engaged and deepens the divide.

Here's what I know: the life you're meant to live is always waiting for you. The question is whether you can tune out the distractions long enough to claim it. There will always be an opportunity. And there will always be an excuse. Which one do you choose?

I'll never forget where I came from or what it took to get here—the pain I suffered, and the pain I caused. At some point, I had to let go of what was out of my control so I could pour my energy into what mattered most. First, into myself. Then, into the people I love and those I aim to impact.

I am liberal. I am conservative. I am independent. I don't belong to any party. I am done with the bullshit. I am committed to working on myself so I can be the change I desire to see in the world.

This isn't to say I pretend to have the answers, but I'm always evolving. I don't want to become one of those people who stops listening because they think they've got it all figured out.

Have you ever seen those funny insurance company commercials where people become their parents? That's not me. I want to stay open even when I disagree with someone, I try to understand their perspective because everyone's just reacting to their own life. What makes sense to one person won't make sense to someone else. "What you eat don't make me shit," as Jay-Z said.

And yeah, corporate corruption is a massive problem. The demand for constant quarterly profits forces companies into behaviors that hurt everyone. Why can't a company just do well, remain solvent, be stable? Because they answer to shareholders, most of whom are rich and anonymous and only care about margins. A company that doesn't look like it's growing loses to the ones that. It's hard to pretend this is a system that serves people. It just protects the elite; it just keeps making the rich richer at the expense of everyone else.

So what are we supposed to do?

Be aware of the world. But if you can't directly control it ... let it go. My awareness of the system being "rigged and unfair" makes no difference. But if I focus on those things I may be inclined to start blaming them too. And I made a commitment to choosing a different path. I'm learning the rules, playing the game, and pushing back where I can in order to build something better. My goal is clear: earn $100 million and give away $100 million. If you asked me just a year ago, I was still struggling with the idea that I may become someone I don't like in pursuit of these lofty goals. However, that was just another story I was telling myself out of fear. So, I began telling myself a different story.

Who is the man I have to become in order for this new version of me to stay true to my roots? We can begin telling ourselves a different story when we start asking ourselves different questions. And I've started asking, *what if I could have a little of both*? What if I could live well, give back, and keep my soul intact?

Now, I know I can be trusted with that kind of wealth and responsibility. Mostly because I've failed enough, hurt enough, and grown enough to know who I am. I know something about where I can make moves to make a real impact.

I know people who are obsessed with wealth and status symbols—the cars, the jets, and all that fancy shit. And they're empty inside. But I'm a little different.

Don't get me wrong. I love luxury. I live in a beautiful home in a safe neighborhood with tree lined streets now. My wife and I drive not one, but two luxury SUVs. I have designer clothes. But my favorite, comfortable outfit to wear from sneakers to my underwear cost less than $200 all in. I love $150 steaks, but I'm just as comfortable eating at Applebee's or staying at a Holiday Inn. I think the difference for me is that I've got perspective and gratitude. I know what it is like to grow up with the bare minimum. And because of my time in prison, I know what it's like to have almost nothing. Ironically, prison was where I started to find myself. Because of this, I know for a fact that money will not change me. As they say, money just enhances who you really are. For good or bad. So yeah, I travel a lot, and I kinda want a jet. I know the hypocrisy. But I also know this train isn't stopping. AI, drones, surveillance, class divides—these days, it's all accelerating. I could waste my life shouting about it, or I could build a life where I do good with what I've been given, maybe even level the playing field a bit for someone else and still enjoy some of the finer things.

Because here's another ugly truth: people born into wealth aren't usually hungry. They're entitled. The American Dream is alive and well for those who have never had a taste of it. Once you have, you start guarding it. That's why so many of these suburban middle-class folks are hardcore (as in, he can do no wrong) Trump die-hards. They feel something's being taken from them, even if they didn't earn it or hustle as much as their parents and grandparents for it. They inherited a sense of entitled safety. Now they're just trying to hold on (and the thing is, most of them don't have all that much, really). I'm no Trumper. I'm just acknowledging that perspective shapes beliefs which shape people's political ideals. In other words, most people are just trying to protect what they have. The poor want more (but stay quiet because they don't have a voice). The wealthy want it all (and get richer as a result). And unfortunately, the middle class pays for most of it. And we all make the mistake that what *we* believe is the truth. You want to know something that is actually true? "There are no facts, only interpretations," as Nietzsche said.

And the unfortunate news is that it's not like there's some utopia waiting on the other side. We have a country full of angry young people who feel like there is little hope for the future and whose minds have been warped by the narratives of their social media feeds. Add to that a group of far-left liberals who embrace socialist and communist ideologies where everyone is equal. I understand why people might adopt this belief system because I've been on the short end of the stick but as someone who has had to work for theirs, I just didn't grow up with the idea that the government was going to come save us. It's just my opinion but If communism or socialism worked, we would have had some great examples to point to already. And just to be clear, The United States is already a mix of capitalism with plenty of Socialism mixed in.

I also don't believe in the "pull yourself up by your bootstraps" myth that staunch conservatives carry. "Some people don't have boots or straps to pull up," as Joe Rogan once said. So, what's right and what's wrong? It depends entirely on how your beliefs are built. Your entire worldview is shaped by your experience.

But that doesn't mean there's no hope.

I still believe in small acts. I still believe in building something with people you trust. I've spent a lot of money finding the right circle. But they're out there—people who do good, who love their families, who give back, and yeah, some of them fly private. They're rare, but they exist.

And I intend to be one of them. Not just for my ego or self-indulgence, but to show my community what is possible.

I may not be there yet, but I'm on my way. I know that the selfishness we're born with can be unlearned. I see it in my kids—how natural it is to snatch a toy just because someone else is playing with it. A bit of envy, greed and selfishness is baked into who we are. But growth means pushing back on that. Growing up means breaking cycles; something I've only learned because I failed.

Because I caused pain. Because the world forced me to look at myself in the mirror and make a different choice.

## Perception is Reality

I still think about Eric Garner from Staten Island, NYC. He was a black man who was killed for selling loose cigarettes in 2014. He had a long arrest record for petty crime, and on that fateful day, he didn't want to go back to jail. He resisted a little; nothing wild, mind you, but the officer jumped on his neck—literally choked him out. And Eric died. On camera. His desperate cries of "I can't breathe" kicked off a national movement.

That moment changed me. That moment changed a lot of people.

And it taught me a lot about perspective. I remember talking to a white male colleague; a chiropractor I did business with. We watched the same video—the same footage, the same events—and I thought it was clear as day: that cop killed him.

But this guy, he goes, "Well, yeah, but they let him up after he said that." And I remember sitting there thinking, *Are you out of your mind?* We just watched the same damn thing, and he'd seen something totally different. Thankfully, I didn't get angry or try to prove my point, but I learned something invaluable at that moment. Mostly because the curious version of me wanted to understand.

That's when it hit me. Two people can watch the exact same scene and walk away with completely different truths. Not because one's lying, but because we all carry our own baggage, our own fears, our own experiences. The shit that shapes how we see everything. It was a realization that helped me find a kind of grace. It taught me not to assume I knew what people believed and that I needed to be a better listener. And honestly, I don't think I'd have learned that lesson if my life hadn't gone sideways the way it did.

So no, I don't romanticize rule-breaking, just like I don't hand out excuses. But I *do* understand what it means to live in the gray, to make hard choices, to be burned, and to walk out with your soul intact. And if I'm going to make a difference in this world, I know it can't just be for me, but for the people that follow. To do that, I've got to remember that everyone's seeing the world through their own lens, and that maybe the only real power we have is how much grace we choose to give.

## Failure is Progress

But doing great things means risking failure.

Failure doesn't always look like falling. Sometimes, it looks like sitting still. Waiting. Playing by the rules and hoping someone else will hand you a break. But most of the time? The system's not designed for you to win.

We talk a lot about fear, as if it's just some inner demon to be conquered. But fear doesn't exist in a vacuum. It's shaped, reinforced, and built into the design of our most important institutions. It's the residue of systems that tell you to stay in line, or else. *Don't rock the boat. Don't dream too loud. Don't ask for more than what's offered.* It's a fear that's learned and enforced.

I felt it when I was working under a boss who owed me fifty grand. He strung me along for weeks...then months. I'd already made the business plan that would change my life, but I stayed. Because as broken as the situation was, the fear of stepping out on my own was worse than the fear of getting burned.

And that's the trap. Fear of the unknown always outweighs the pain we already know.

It took betrayal to wake me up. In retrospect, getting screwed was the best thing that ever happened to me. Because at that moment, I finally moved. I *finally* took action because I had had enough. And once I did? That fear started to shrink, and the pieces started falling into place.

That's the trick about fear: it never leaves. But the more you move through it, the less power it has. And the system? It *wants* you afraid. Because if you're afraid, you'll accept the deal. You'll take the scraps. You'll follow the rules—especially the ones that are only there to keep you small.

Since then, I've been through lawsuits, audits, and all the stress and bullshit that comes along with those experiences. I've lost close to two million dollars over the last couple of years through settlements, forfeited receivables, and legal fees—most of it triggered by just the suggestion of wrongdoing. Just the word *fraud*, whispered in the right ears, can kick off a whole machinery of reprisal. Because the rules aren't about truth—they're about control.

And the people with the power? They know how to use those rules.

So yeah, I pushed back. I pushed hard because I've lived the alternative. I've seen how easily someone with vision, with drive and integrity, can be sidelined by a system designed to grind them down. You can follow all the rules and somehow still lose. You can do the right thing and still end up behind.

This is why so many people never try. Not because they lack courage, but because they've been taught, subtly and persistently, that failure will not be forgiven.

You don't leap until you learn that this isn't true. You don't grow until you risk something real. I used to stress over $1,000 problems—now I can make a $5 million decision with less fear than that old version of me who was afraid to go big. That confidence didn't come from success. It came from taking chances on myself after having to push through my own fears and insecurities. That confidence: it came from wins. But the failures ultimately taught me much more and made the wins that much sweeter.

So no, don't just break rules for the thrill of it. Break rules when the rules are bullshit. When they're designed to keep people down. There can be a cost, but in the end, it doesn't matter how obedient you are, because the game is still rigged.

**Growth Under Fire**

It's funny how often the rules we're told to follow started with noble intentions. Insurance, for example, began within religious communities as a means to care for widows when their husbands died. But somewhere along the way, someone realized: *Wait—they're just going to give me the money, and I get to hold onto it?*

That's all it took. Now it's a cash cow. Big companies like GEICO, The Hartford, Liberty Mutual rake in billions while only paying out a fraction of what they take in. These companies aren't about protection anymore—they're about profit. They're not about trust—they're about leverage.

And the same goes for housing. Landlords who can't evict tenants even when they're being gamed by the system still have to pay the bank. Housing markets explode as hedge funds buy up stock, blocking huge swaths of people from the hope of stable housing. We talk a lot about justice, but rarely do we ask: justice for who? We build policies intended to protect people from harm, but then we let those same policies become weapons in un-scrupulous hands.

So again—whose rules? And who do they serve?

That's why I don't apologize for the way I do things. I trust that my intentions are good, be-cause I've seen how ugly this world can be, and I still want to play my part in making it better. I've got a lot of work left to do, but that's my mission, and I believe I can be trusted with it. I've been shaped by too many hard lessons to do anything else.

**In Summary:**

- You don't need a perfect plan to start—just a clear goal and the guts to be-gin. Clarity comes through motion.

- Many institutional rules protect power, not people. Breaking them isn't rebel-lion—it's survival, as long as your intent is just.

- Institutions train you to fear failure, so you'll stay small. But staying still is just another kind of falling.

- Breaking rules doesn't mean abandoning ethics. The golden rule still applies—move fast but move with care.

- Failure, betrayal, and pressure reveal who you really are—and who you're becoming. Let them shape you, not break you.

5

# RELATIONSHIP CAPITAL

## Only You Can Create the World You Want

No relationship is more important than the relationship that you have with yourself. Not only does it condition what you decide is possible, but it also dictates the shape of all of the other relationships you'll have in your life. How you create and cultivate relationship capital—who you associate with, the mentors you embrace, and the media you consume is essential to building the life you want. And as you execute on your plans, how you work on one reinforces how you cultivate the other.

You've heard it said in a million places and in a million different ways: how can you love another if you don't love yourself? There's so much truth to that. How can you be a teacher if you refuse to learn anything new? How can you be successful if you have not seen, touched, or been influenced by those who have found success? It's important that you surround yourself with people who can reflect back the world you want to make for yourself.

So many of us grow up in settings that, either through conscious or unconscious projection, are limited by what the people around us think is "realistic." Sometimes, the people closest to us limit us because, to them, doing something exceptional is inherently unrealistic. They dismiss our dreams as being unattainable almost by reflex. Parents are frequently the main culprits here. They subconsciously kneecap their own children, convincing their kids that they aren't capable of accomplish-

ing important things because they never succeed-
ed in breaking through themselves.

I say this because I've run into this many times
before. In fact, it's to the point that I implore kids
I speak to, especially high school aged kids and
young adults, to dream big and to dream without
these limitations. I also encourage them to protect those dreams by being extremely selective of
who they share them with. I mean, there's always
someone at the career day or someone important
to them who insists that they not dream too big,
that they have a backup plan. To learn a trade or do
something more "feasible." But the truth is that
these warnings are a reflection of that person's
limitations, placed in your subconscious mind,
and not of what you are truly capable of.

One of the great tragedies of life is that so many
of us follow the lead of small thinkers and end up
becoming small thinkers in turn.

## Get Around BIG Thinkers

I mentioned it earlier, but my mother's advice to me, "If you think you can, you can; if you think you can't, you can't. Either way, you're right," still guides a lot of my thinking. She was a social worker who might never have dreamt so grand as I dared to, but she would use this mantra to help me find the faith I needed to take control of my own destiny.

That simple phrase wasn't hers. As far as I know, it was something Henry Ford used to say. But the meaning was always clear: you are the end all and be all of the outcomes you manifest in your life. Sure, there'll be plenty of twists in the road. Unforeseen, unwanted things that are going to knock you right on your ass, but it's ultimately you and only you that allows those things to keep you down. If you stay down, that's on you. It's your responsibility to get back up and try again.

But you don't have to do it alone. My own experience has been a bit of a testament to this truth. By surrounding myself with winners, with people that absolutely believe that they can become the masters of their own fates, I have been lift-ed up in countless ways. You see, when you sur-round yourself with small thinkers, people that only talk about other people, or people that only denigrate others, you become smaller yourself. Small thinkers don't discuss ideas; they don't have vision. Instead, they concentrate on pulling you down to their level. It's almost beyond them to support you, believe in you, and to help push you towards the enormous goals you want to set for yourself. Small thinkers will tell you this is just being "realistic." They'll tell you to have a backup plan.

It's all bullshit. They're just trying to excuse their own failings and fears.

## People Are Your Greatest Resource

Relationship capital is about the people who shape your life. Sure, some of the world's most successful individuals have risen from humble be-ginnings, but that's because they built a circle that set them up for success—family, early mentors, and eventually selectively chosen peers—that could give them a leg up.

Let's be clear: "networking" isn't just a buzzword. It needs to become a way of life. The hard truth is that you can't achieve greatness on your own. No one is truly 'self-made." And no one person can teach you everything. When you're young, your options can be limited to your parents, teachers, and whatever mentors might enter your orbit. As an adult, you can be more proactive. You can start choosing the people you want to learn from. Your journey to success starts when you recognize that you have the power to choose new allies—people who not only dream big (like you) but also know how to put in the work. You can align yourself with doers who push you forward, who don't shy away from taking on challenges and aren't afraid to share their hard-won lessons.

There's a common misconception that success must come at the *expense* of others. Beliefs like money being the root of all evil, and that every rich guy got there by cheating someone out of something can really hold us up. Anyone who's really climbed the ladder knows these are myths. Real success comes from hard work, smart choices, and yes, the willingness to learn from those who have been there before. You've probably heard that money just makes you more of who you truly are. So sure, if you're an asshole, you may become a rich asshole. But if you're compassionate, thoughtful and generous... well, you get the point.

So, when you build your network with intention—choosing those who push you to be the best version of yourself—you're not just collecting contacts. You're cultivating relationship capital, a powerful resource that can help you overcome obstacles and reach your dreams. It's raw, it's real, and it's essential if you're serious about climbing to the top.

And you'll know when things start to change. When you start making progress, you often notice a shift in your circle of trust. People who once supported you might suddenly become cold or even negative, claiming you're somehow different. Or they'll start accusing you of "selling out." That's not because you're losing touch. It's because your progress challenges their reliance on their own limitations. It's a natural reaction when you choose to surround yourself with winners, you're going to push people away who don't share that energy. You'll learn quickly who's with you and who's holding you back.

## Work on You

There are lots of ways to grow a quality network both In person and digitally. Ironically, network growth starts with subtraction and not addition. Who are the people that you're wasting your precious time and energy on? They're not going to be the ones that help you move ahead, so feel free to lose a few numbers.

Let's keep it simple. I want you to start by looking at your social media feed. Take a close look at what you're "following" and eliminate all the garbage that doesn't feed your belief, positivity, or provide the tools, knowledge, and words of wisdom that build you up and make you smarter.

Most people can probably drop 90% of the pages that they're following. Almost none of them will make their lives any more fruitful. Brand names, celebrities, and all that self-promotional junk we acquire; most of it can go. Instead, surround your virtual self with positivity: motivational pages, entrepreneurship pages, and thought leaders in your industry (or the industry you're drawn to). If you're into real estate, follow real estate pages; if you're into fitness, follow fitness pages; if you're into history, follow history pages.

I want to offer you a hard truth. If you're someone who follows celebrities, sports figures, entertainment pages, and all the gossip around those industries, then you're simply watching others live out their dreams while sapping the time you could be spending building yours. Surrounding yourself with the information that will help you grow is just as important as surrounding yourself with a group of people that want to see you win. And it's a really easy way to cultivate your talent and your passion.

And let's be honest: when you first start out, you may not have much in the way of resources. Don't let that deter you. There's plenty of virtual resources, stuff like online workshops and Meet-Up groups that can provide opportunities to start growing your network and connecting with opportunities. And when you can afford to get into a room, just start small and keep pushing until you can get into a bigger room, then a bigger room, and an even bigger room.

And don't be a cheapskate. Never forget you are the best investment you can ever make. There's no stock or bond, there's no fucking crypto coin; there's no business that's ever going offer a better return on investment than the ones you make in yourself. Invest in your mind, in your self-belief, and in your body. Work with coaches to help in every facet of your life, whether for your mind and mindset, for your physical health, for your relationships, for your spiritual well-being. There are pastors if Christ is your bag; there's monks and yogis if you're a Buddhist or a meditation junkie. And lastly, there's always YouTube for those with limited means. If you don't have much in the way of resources, then it's on you to be more resourceful. Instead of saying that you don't have the money to do something, ask yourself how can a person with no money get started anyways?

There are experts in every walk of life who make their living sharing their perspective. So really, if you want to be better, why not drop a little money on access to the people that are well versed in the thing that you're trying to accomplish? There are podcasts, free audio books and an endless supply of informative resources that are free and can be accessed through a simple search.

## Masterminds

One of the most powerful resources I have discovered are Masterminds (A catch phrase for Summits, Conferences or Seminars led by experts) The term "mastermind" was coined by Dale Carnegie in his book *Think and Grow Rich*. In it, Carnegie interviews a "who's who" of contemporary entrepreneurs and changemakers whom he called "masterminds." Dale understood that the most successful people in the world were often successful for the same reasons, and that in order to get ahead in life there was no need to reinvent the wheel. You could just as well find the people that had already done what you want to do and learn from them directly.

Masterminds are events hosted by the experts that drive industries and draw communities of like-minded innovators to themselves. To get close to these people, you may have to travel. You may have to pay for airfare, you may have to pay for a hotel, and you're going to have to pay to get in the room. But if you can get the money, I implore you to attend some. And if you can't manage all of that, there are plenty of virtual masterminds that don't require travel either.

And the investment is totally worth it. Think about it: We're quick to hand over fifty, sixty, seventy or even one hundred thousand dollars a year for a college degree. Even those with limited means can entertain the idea of attending a state, city, or even online university. Also consider community college, which I personally consider to be the best value in higher education (because I'm a product of one, I may be biased). But for anyone who doesn't see college as a viable option or just knows that it isn't for them, there are plenty of mastermind programs that offer financing options as well. And they may even be the better option. Masterminds, after all, connect us *directly* to the people who shape industries. They get you plugged in, not just warmed up.

But whatever you do, don't skimp on your own development. This kind of short-sighted thinking is the biggest mistake that doomed entrepreneurs make: they don't surround themselves with the people that are already winning in the game that they're trying to win at. They don't invest in themselves and in quality connections. It's asinine, and the reason it's asinine is because they think they can do everything on their own. They think they can be the bookkeeper; they want to be the accountant; they want to be a marketing rep. Maybe they think that they can do everything better than everybody else, but more likely than not they're just being cheap because they have yet to truly learn to value their time. The fact is you need to build a team. You need relationships and the relationship capital they bring. Relationship capital is what's going to catapult you into the stratosphere. And masterminds are the best hack to quickly build the most effective relationships. The quicker you can get on the mastermind train, the faster you'll get to the place you want to be.

Because what we think about is what we get and who we surround ourselves with is who we become.

## In Summary

- Your mindset determines your possibilities and relationships. Avoid internalizing limiting beliefs from others.

- Don't be afraid to think big. Accordingly, surround yourself with ambitious people who lift you up, not those who hold you back.

- Success comes from aligning with doers and mentors who can help you master your craft.

- Prioritize learning, mentorship, and personal growth to accelerate success. Don't be afraid to drop a little money on these things.

**6**

# ELIMINATE BLAME AND TAKE BACK YOUR POWER

## The Future is Bright

We live in an age of miracles, and everything you need is suddenly at your fingertips. You have these amazing things called the Internet and Artificial Intelligence at your disposal. Think about it... just 30 years ago you'd be stuck rifling off through 26 editions of an encyclopedia, going to the library, doing all kinds of research, going and getting microfilm on old news stories just to get some basic background on an opportunity. Today, you can spend an hour or two with Google and Chat GPT and probably learn even more.

I mean, this generation has it easier than it's ever been, yet somehow, so many of these miracles just make it easier for them to complain. Don't chalk my attitude around this to me being a little bit older than the people that might be reading this book. Chalk it up to the fact that I've now lived through six different decades: the 70s, 80s, 90s, 2000s, 2010s, and now the 2020s. At this point, I really am starting to feel like I've seen it all.

So I'm going off my own experience: I've seen the world change dramatically. After all, when I was a teenager, cell phones were just being invented, and the internet wasn't even a thing. Now, 20 years later, everyone's got that tech in their pockets. And we're all online. All of the time. With so much available to us, with so many unfolding possibilities, all that's left to ask is what are you using it for?

Most people just use these things to kill time, keeping themselves entertained while the masters overseeing our social media ecosystems herd users like sheep. This probably accounts, at least in part, for why so many people hurl blame at these systems for all their failures and shortcomings. Looked at a certain way, it's almost as if the masses don't have a choice anymore. Well, I've got good news for you. Because you can *know* what these systems are doing to you, you can take back your power and turn these systems back on themselves. But doing so starts by being honest about your culpability for your attachment to these systems. When you find yourself surrounded by negativity and struggling with your sense of victimization, I've found that empowerment begins with two simple words: MY BAD. Hear me out.

Once you can take responsibility for what's happening *to* you, you can actually flip that narrative on its head and learn to tell yourself that it's happening *for* you. No matter how bad things get, no matter how tragic the present might seem, no matter how devastating the future might look, no matter how serious a loss you may have suffered, you have the power to reframe your experiences and use it to fuel your push forward. But doing so is a choice, and it's gotta be a conscious one.

## Blame is Worthless

Blame drives a lot of people in today's society. It seems like so many of us are always looking for someone to blame: *It's the government. Someone did this to me. I'm sad because of social media. It's my parents. If only they were paying me more money at this job I hate. The education system is rigged. The health care system is rigged. Society is rigged. The world is rigged.*

Well, I've got news for you. Life is unfair. It never has been. And it never will be. The entire concept of fairness is ridiculous. Just look at nature as an example. Simply put, survival of the fittest is the law the world follows. Fairness is a uniquely human concept. And I am here to tell you that it doesn't exist. The sooner that you can embrace that basic truth, the sooner you will be on your way to strengthening your own resolve and putting in the work that's going to get you where you want to go. And here's the thing: When you accept that the world is unfair, it's easier to let go of the idea that you're a target. Letting go of that feeling is important because, if you're going to build and maintain your confidence, you've got to learn to master the art of letting go of blame and shame.

For all the trouble it causes, blame is a psychological crutch. Blaming the world; convincing ourselves that our struggles aren't really our problem is just an easy way to fail and use the fact that the world is unfair to stay in whatever comfortable rut we've gotten stuck in.

But I've got news. In a lot of ways, you're probably better off today than at any time in the past, and the world is actually fairer than it ever has been. There are still some pretty important inequities out there, but I'd like to propose that there's never been an easier time to succeed. And because of technology, information and knowledge it has never been easier for anyone to access opportunity.

## Check Yourself

Now, I'll grant you: Shifting your perspective around this doesn't just happen. You've got to make an active choice; one that you make based on the facts of your own experience. And I won't pretend it's easy. After all, there's just so much confusion in the world today. All the distraction really does make it easier to blame than to uncover the layers of your own shortcomings, misgivings, or to really suss out the roots of your inability to take your power back. It really is easier to simply toss around blame and use it as a crutch. The traps are real. But so are the tools that can liberate you from them.

As a young man growing up in a housing project with a working single mom, I held on to a belief that the government was unfair, that the world was out to get people of color and the poor. A lot of us were raised to believe that the inequities we suffered growing up were all imposed by some higher power that wanted us to suffer. But as I grew up, I learned the truth: it's all bullshit. This story we'd tell about being victims was just that. A story.

I don't say this to suggest that there aren't important inequities in the United States. There absolutely are. They exist in every city and every community across America and around the world. Was there victimization of people of color in the past? 100%! Is it still happening today? Absolutely. Racism and bias are alive and well in America. So, I'm no fool; I'm not trying to deny reality. But living in blame will never get you anywhere. And this book is about empowering you to go beyond blame. I mean, let's be real. The system is rigged in favor of people who already have power and access; that's how they stay there. You can't count on any of that coming undone, so stop holding your breath. And stop bitching and complaining. Unless you're doing something to actively make things better. Systemic change takes generations, and you can't afford to wait. Take charge of your life, push your limits, and be the change you want to see. After all, what's easier to change? The systems of the world, or your response to them?

Making this change isn't always easy to do, of course. In my experience, the only way to take back that power is to learn to take back control of your blame. Because the truth is, if you're stewing in blame and resentment, then you're going to stay exactly where you are right now. To escape, you have to recognize your culpability in the systems that have a hold on you.

Now most people don't do this, and the mental health crisis that's gripped so much of the world is, I think, a direct consequence of it. Don't get me wrong. There's never been a shortage of mental health issues out there, but many of them are accentuated by technology, the rise of helicopter parenting, and the various challenges that plague modern civilization. But despite all that, there's no greater force than the power of your own mind and your own will power. You can overcome these challenges if you adopt the right frame of mind. And taking back blame is an integral part in how you empower yourself to handle the challenges that life will inevitably throw at you.

## The Way Out is Through

Not to say I didn't have to figure this out in my own life. As a young man, I often blamed external forces: the presidency, the government, the Republicans or the Democrats, depending on who was in power. But I came to realize that none of these things had more influence over my outcomes than my own attitude. But I really do think it's important to stress that you don't have to beat yourself up; don't be any harder on yourself than you have to be. I just want you to stop letting blame hold you back.

After all, in today's world, so much of our political division, so much of the chaos we experience is, in fact, stoked by the media companies and the framing of our feeds. I'm not ignorant of the fact that people are being manipulated by the media, both social and traditional. But again, if you know this and decide to fall in line with the story of unfairness and blame and doubt they promote…well, at some point, that's on you. Turn the narrative on its head and take back your power.

Start by asking yourself: Why do I think this is happening? What's the story in my head? What can I do to turn that narrative around? What can I do to make myself feel better? What can I do to empower myself? What are the tools available to me?

And there's a few. In addition to reshaping how you manage blame, focus on movement. Movement is one of the most important things that we can embrace to get our life, well, moving. We need to move out of the space that the story looping in our head is keeping us in. When you feel stuck on the couch, or trapped in an endless Netflix hole, just get up and move. Otherwise, those hours and hours turn into days and days, and then into weeks, months, and years. If you're not careful, by the time you think to look back, you'll find that you've lost huge chunks of your life.

But it doesn't stop there. Next you want to start working on how you can forgive yourself for having lost sight of your possibility. Forgiveness is an incredibly potent tool and is always at your disposal if we use it properly. Forgiveness is how we clear and resolve the blame we carry for ourselves and for others. Which means it has to work both ways. When someone does you wrong, your emotions are going to be running hot. You might feel furious or resentful. When this happens, remember to breathe before you act. Because when the dust settles and your anger subsides, try your damnedest to forgive whoever did it to you. Whatever happened to throw you off, forgiveness is an essential component of how you move forward. After all, we've all been on the wrong side at some point in our lives.

I mean, take a moment to think about some time that someone did you wrong. Was it your anger and resentment, your negative thoughts and projections that got you to a better place? Of course not. Those emotions are crippling. Holding on to them serves you not at all. If you're going to live your best life, you've got to get anger out of the way nice and quick.

And so, it is with all our negative emotions. They can trap us, leaving us tangled up like a fish in a net. Once you're stuck in that thing, you've got to be smart, cool, and collected. Otherwise, all that fighting is just going to leave you stuck and sinking.

So, learn to let go of your anger and resentment. Otherwise, your ass is going to drown.

## Emotional Intelligence vs Emotional Fitness

I'm all too familiar with the shame that comes with not forgiving yourself. Between that and my sense of blame, I spent a lot of my early years just straight up not giving a fuck. I was just serving my own selfish interests.

Eventually this thinking caught up with me in a big way. That's how I landed myself in prison at the age of 29. Looking back, I made a series of bad decisions that came out of my anger and blame, that kept me from fully taking responsibility for the life I was leading. Maybe it's ironic that prison taught me the emotional intelligence that I was lacking all along. The lessons that I had to learn there would turn out to be the best thing that ever happened to me. But you know, I think it helped a lot that I *chose* to frame the experience that way.

One of the most important things I learned in prison was the difference between emotional intelligence and emotional fitness. Emotional intelligence is a lot like emotional awareness, you know, being able to name your feelings and recognize them when they come up. Emotional fitness, however, was something that would take me another decade and a half to develop. Emotional fitness is our ability to not just identify and understand our emotions, but to understand and control how we react to emotional stimuli. Once we have learned to not let the things that happen to us rattle us or knock us off course, this is where mastery starts.

The important thing is this: What we decide to make of our circumstances is the best way to empower us to shape our future. You see, it's not that prison was the best thing that could have happened to me—there's nothing good about going to prison. But because I took the opportunity to shift my perspective about my situation a lot of pieces fell into place. If nothing else, it helped me get clear on the life I wanted to build when I returned home. I knew that I needed to make some pretty big changes to be the best man I could. So, free from distractions and outside bullshit, I buckled down and did the work.

Moreover, cut off from drugs and alcohol, I started to craft the narrative of who "Sean" would become after I got out. For me, change started with the words "my fault" and became real when I forgave myself.

But that came later.

## Forgiveness and Grace

None of this happened overnight. Prison might have started the process, but I didn't forgive myself for decades. I held on to the embarrassment I'd caused my mom, my family, and myself for years and years. While I was working through that, I started my own business and was (on paper) doing pretty well for myself. I mean, shit was all going great. But inside I was still broken. I still wasn't the man that I would become because I was still carrying all that shame and that guilt.

Overcoming that took me years of therapy and counseling. It also took me getting sober in 2022. That's when I finally got the clarity I needed and started working on myself. A major breakthrough came when I attended an early Mastermind. The other men there were like brothers, and they gave me the space to share my story, real and raw, with a community that didn't judge me for what I'd done, the pain I'd caused or the hurt that I was going through. With their support, I was able to overcome all that shame and guilt and finally start to take full control of my life.

I also think it helps when you start to believe in something greater than yourself; whatever you call it. Yes, I know it might sound a little woo-woo to recommend God or some other universal spirit; Buddha, Shiva, Jesus, or whatever. It really doesn't matter what you call it, just that you tap into the spirit of an omnipotence that loves you more than you can love yourself. Knowing that God or The Universe loves you and is actually designed for you to win opens you up to the possibility that you can truly love yourself and others.

I don't know your story, of course. But it's a safe bet that if you're still reading this book, you're probably holding on to some things that are hindering you. Letting go of these isn't an overnight process, but it is possible. And we all deserve the life that awaits us on the other side of blame, guilt, and shame. To get there, first you've got to be willing to start down the road of healing yourself.

Only then will you truly be able to call up the reserves you need to share that grace with others. So take responsibility. First for yourself, and then for your attitudes towards others. Be honest about the blame to escape the shame, then you can open that space up to everyone else.

## In Summary

- The world is full of opportunities, but success starts with personal responsibility. Stop blaming external forces and take control of your own narrative.

- Blaming others keeps you stuck, and shame drains your power. Let go, accept life's unfairness, and focus on what you *can* change.

- Change requires movement, mindset shifts, and self-reflection. Forgiveness—of yourself and others—is key to breaking free from negativity.

- True transformation happens when you release past burdens, embrace self-for-giveness, and open yourself to something bigger than just you.

# 7

# HEALTH IS WEALTH

## Identity and Health

I've struggled with weight all of my life. I spent most of it heavy and long identified as the fat kid I grew up considering myself. My mother would lovingly call me "husky," but she was just being nice: I was fat. Somewhere early on, overeating had become my main tool for managing stress. It was a habit that helped me hit 350 pounds not once, but twice. Because of my yo-yoing weight, over the years I've lost over a ton.

Being so heavy meant that I always carried a sense that I needed to get the weight off. The first time

I had some real success was in the summer before my senior year of high school. That summer of basketball was the spark. But over time I learned that sustainable transformation isn't just about going all out until you drop; it's about building strength, improving your overall health, and aligning your habits with your biology. Movement is the starting point, not the full picture. I wasn't tracking calories or logging meals, but I was moving daily, eating whole foods, and cutting processed junk. Those consistent choices naturally reduced my intake without me obsessing over numbers. You don't always need a spreadsheet, but you do need structure. More importantly, I saw the way that people treated me start to change. Especially the girls—girls who'd never noticed me before suddenly did. The difference was pretty stark.

See, losing weight changed more than just my body. It changed my attitude. I felt better both physically and mentally. And when you feel better about yourself, all kinds of things fall into place.

When you like what you see in the mirror, the world feels different. After all, many of our personal struggles are internal; the same is true of our triumphs.

I'd grown up struggling to maintain a positive body image. I had terrible acne until about sophomore year of high school, a pretty bad case of "pizza face." It was a sight. I'm feeling a little trauma come back even as I write about it. Ewwww.

On top of that, I developed gynecomastia, a buildup of fatty tissue on the chest, more commonly known as "man boobs." I eventually had surgery to remove it in my mid 20s. But you can imagine the added layer of insecurity. All of this conspired to leave me with a generally poor body image. I'd see myself in the mirror and still see flaws, whatever progress I might have made.

The biggest shift wasn't in my body—it was in how I was challenged to see myself. I stopped chasing 6-12 week transformations and instead focused on becoming an example for my kids. But identity isn't just mental. It's built through action. Every time I trained when I didn't feel like it, chose real food over comfort food, went for a walk, jumped in a sauna or stepped into cold exposure, I was teaching myself who I was becoming. These are the small things that over time compound to a healthier life. The wins are made in the small decisions that can move you forward or keep you stuck.

It took a long time for me to understand that your identity, your sense of self, has to shift if you want change to stick. In my younger days, I knew nothing about nutrition. Growing up in the projects, you couldn't just run to the corner store for a healthy snack. Junk food was everywhere, and the best you could do for a "healthy" option might just be "fresh fruit" at the corner grocery store. A few bananas, platanos (plantains) and an apple if you were lucky. My mom didn't really know any better either. In our house, Caribbean-style cooking was the norm: foods fried in vegetable or corn oil; rice and beans every day. Rice and beans are a staple in many cultures, and can absolutely be part of a healthy diet, especially if you're active.

We also ate chicken, steak (well well done), meatloaf, Italian style home cooking, and a bunch of other mom created goodness. She was actually an excellent chef and would refer to her James Beard cookbook whenever she felt creative or needed a refresher on an older dish. The issue wasn't the carbs or the meats themselves, but the way we prepared them—cooking everything in corn oil, without understanding how these oils, processed foods, and carbs can certainly backfire if your physical demands don't require their presence on your plate. When they do, carbs can be an exceptional tool towards becoming a healthier you!

I also believe that when it comes to weight loss, identity is huge. A person who sees themselves as fit tends to eat like a fit person. I once worked with this tall, thin colleague who reminded me of Squidward from *SpongeBob*. But that's neither here. Nor there. We went out with some other colleagues one night and he ordered soup for dinner.

That was it. I couldn't imagine being satisfied with that, but that's how he saw himself, as someone who eats light.

And that's the difference. If you identify as "the fat kid" or "the person who just loves to eat," you're going to act accordingly. Comedians joke about it all the time: the big person who says, "I don't eat that much," but come 11 p.m., they're raiding the fridge and binging at the worst time possible for their body. I think we've all known people who swear they barely eat and yet are dangerously obese. They are ashamed. I know. Because I was too. And as ridiculous as the notion of an overweight person saying they don't even eat that much sounds, they hold onto it tightly. Something in this all comes back to mindset.

Health is wealth, but it's also knowledge, access, and identity. Until you change all three, you'll never really be able to take control.

## Finding Healthier Habits

I grew up in a food desert, but that wasn't the only part of the environment working against me. I later learned that we lived under harsh lights, stayed up late, and had no access to green space or sunlight in the morning, all of which can impact health. Our biology was being shaped by the entire environment, not just what was in the fridge. I had friends—especially those from West Indian and Caribbean families—who ate whole foods, but for us, that wasn't the norm. Healthy food wasn't just scarce, it was misunderstood. We knew what not to eat, but had no idea what to add in. Things like minerals, fiber, protein, and micronutrients weren't even part of the conversation—and that's what really matters when you want to rebuild your body.

So, the options weren't there, and even when they were, the education wasn't. If you know what to look for, you might walk the extra block and spend the extra couple bucks for decent vegetables and healthier starches. But if you don't understand the long-term ramifications of unhealthy eating, you just buy what's in front of you. And in my neighborhood, what was in front of you was usually fried, processed and pre-packaged garbage.

Growing up poor introduces its own challenges. After all, eating healthy is more expensive, in marginalized neighborhoods especially. And anyways, processed food ships easily, stores forever, and is generally what fills the shelves of corner convenience stores. Fresh food on the other hand? Well, it goes bad relatively quickly. This problem lingers a bit for me even now. My wife will often buy fresh produce for the house, only to have to throw it out a week later because we didn't get through it in time.

Not long after losing all that weight in high school, I slipped back into the old habits. I went back to the same internal thermostat setting, which was apparently set to "fat." I've had to come to terms with that. Even today, when I'm the healthiest I've ever been; even after a couple surgeries to repair some of the damage done over the years, I still catch myself thinking about myself as "the fat kid." But I'm doing better—I've surrounded myself with people who know better, I've educated myself, and I have the resources to eat well even when I'm busy. But I didn't start thinking about nutrition in any meaningful way until my late twenties.

Before I started taking it seriously, I was hovering around 280–300 pounds. That's when I started at Bronx Community College But it wasn't until I transferred to Ithaca College that things got worse. The campus meal plan was basically an all-you-can-eat buffet. Add in all the late-night food runs and regular weed smoking, and I ballooned up to 350 pounds.

I lost it eventually. After graduation, I stayed in Ithaca that summer, enjoying cheap rent, a girlfriend, and plenty of free time. I got some space to start cleaning up my habits. I started to cook my own food because I couldn't afford to eat out. I ran every day, spent time in nature, and started eating massive amounts of fruit and whole foods. Around that time, I also found *Body for Life* by

Bill Phillips; this book proved to be a game changer. His short, strategic full body workouts were simple and effective. But I'd done a lot of damage to my body and was always in danger of putting the weight back on.

A decade later, I found myself back in the same patterns. I'd lose a massive amount of weight, get comfortable, and backslide. Then I'd feel miserable about myself and eat in order to feel better. It was what they call a spiral. Food made me comfortable, then it made me feel guilty. I didn't know it then, but I'd become what's known as an "emotional eater." But I'd catch myself eventually, turn it around, and go hard in the other direction. At one point I tried shortcuts: fat burners, meal replacements, quick hacks. But none of that stuff worked until I got my sleep, movement, and food in order. Supplements don't override bad habits. They only work if your daily rhythm is already aligned with who you want to become. Regardless, I continued through a series of massive swings. Because without real guidance or training in the shifting of my identity, I was just fighting the tide. And the tide was always winning.

## Establish a Better Mindset

If I had to give advice now? Mindset first, diet second. If food is your comfort, you have to understand why that is before you can really escape the habits that result. And you have to escape the expectation that your weight-loss journey will bring instant results. In the first few weeks, you won't see much. Six weeks? You might start to notice some change. But by twelve weeks? The changes will start to become apparent. The funny thing is, you might not really notice the changes yourself. After all, you see yourself every day. But when someone else notices? That's a great feeling.

That's also why I'm torn on weighing yourself daily while building up better habits. For some, checking in regularly can help keep you accountable. For others, at least in the beginning, this can be demoralizing. Remember: that number will bounce up and down for a dozen reasons—water retention, muscle gain, or something to do with what you ate the night before. This can induce the kind of stress that makes people self-sabotage by chasing a lower number instead of focusing on the bigger picture.

If you're disciplined about it, weighing yourself every day can help keep you within a healthy range. You go up a couple pounds, you make adjustments, and you can usually hold steady. But most people—me included—stop stepping on the scale when we know we've been on a binge. You don't want to face the number. You just want to enjoy the food and the mood you're in.

The thing is that a lot of eating has nothing to do with hunger. We eat out of boredom. We eat out of depression. We eat because we're not moving enough. I've been that guy more times than I can count. And weight loss isn't linear. There's a graph out there that shows it perfectly—the line doesn't just slope down. It zigzags, loops, spikes. You retain water. You have a couple of big weekends. You drink. Your weight can bounce all over the place.

So, you have to give yourself some grace. The real shift happens when you can say, "I'm being healthy right now." I'm taking a walk while I'm on this call—that's a healthy move. I'm drinking water instead of soda. Even when I drink Coke Zero, I could beat myself up over the chemical sweeteners, or I could say, "At least I'm not drinking a Coke with high-fructose corn syrup and chasing it with a bag of chips."

That's why it's important to keep perspective. I don't think we have to be over the top about these things. People should feel some freedom to reward themselves. Food is a comfort, and an art, and a profoundly important means of facilitating connection. There's nothing wrong with enjoying it in the right context. Some of the best moments in life happen over a good meal with good company, something that's been true since our ancestors sat around fires telling stories. You can't deny all the joy of eating and expect to be happy. And if all you ever eat is steamed chicken and salad, you're not going to convince me you're living your best life.

Moderation and self-control are key. There's no need to be self-mortifying.

## The Whole Picture

Real, holistic health isn't just about what you eat or how often you hit the gym. It's about everything you take in. Your health is impacted by a lot: the information you consume, the conversations you have, and the media you watch can shape how you see yourself and how you feel. Being conscious of these things are essential to building healthy habits; the earlier the better.

In our information-saturated world, it's hard not to compare yourself to others. Women might have it the hardest, but men are also prone to being made to feel insecure by America's cult of appearance-obsessed celebrity. Personally, I manage mine pretty well. Sure, I've seen guys with great physiques and thought, "Yeah, I'd like to look like that," but I don't live in the comparison game. I don't think it's healthy; not everybody can maintain the same outcomes and we don't all have the time, money, and access.

And I have to recognize that I can't entirely escape my past. I had weight-loss skin-removal surgery at the beginning of 2024. Over the course of my life, I'd been through too many cycles of expansion and contraction from big weight swings. My collagen had lost its elasticity, so it couldn't tighten up like it might for someone who'd only had to lose fifty pounds once upon a time. As a result, my loose skin made me extremely insecure. So, I had to have it removed, which helped build a ton of confidence. It was as if I was leaving the old me in the past.

The lesson here is this: if you're a younger person reading this book, start to build some healthy habits now. Because I spent so much of my life overweight, I've had to manage other consequences I wouldn't have otherwise. I've got some skeletal and joint issues that hold me back and pop up as recurring injuries, consequences of having carried all that extra weight for so many years. If you're closer to my age, it's important not to let your past stop you from embracing change. In my case, I focus on how far I've come and on how I can maintain the gains that I've made. I mean, I'd be lying if I said I was completely comfortable though. I'm still hesitant to take my shirt off at the beach. Not because of loose skin but now because of the scars I got as a result of removing it. I'll wear a tank top, maybe a t-shirt, and I save the shirtless moments for when I'm with people I know well. It just goes to show that as far as I've come, I guess that sometimes I still feel like that fat kid.

And maybe I do compare myself to others more than I like to admit. I do worry about how people see me. Like anyone else, I like to think of myself as a decent looking guy, and that means comparing myself to some pretty rigid baselines. But you can't let these feelings run your life. Some guys get stuck in that cycle, picking themselves apart in the mirror. I've learned not to do that. You should too. Don't spiral out in front of the bathroom mirror every day—focus on being *your* best self, not someone else's.

## Maintaining My Progress

As for what works for me now? Weight training, stretching and occasional Yoga and a lot of walking. Walking is the most underrated exercise you can do. The key thing is always to make sure you're getting something in every day. After all, movement is medicine. Whether you're overweight or not, getting in some movement will also lift your mood. Too many people think exercise is only about weight loss—they forget how good it makes you feel in the moment.

If you're in a tough spot, use movement as an anchor. Ten minutes on a treadmill. A walk around the block. Air squats in your living room. Resistance training—with weights or just your body—forces you into a conversation between your body and your mind. Every rep builds strength, not just in your muscles, but in your belief that you can do hard things.

Of course, I also love the gym. Always have. Lifting weights is my anchor. I like lifting heavy, pushing myself, and seeing progress week after week. I track everything in an app so I can look back at what I lifted last time and try to beat it. But at 47, I've had to face reality. I can't throw weights around like I used to, but I can strive to maintain my gains.

As you do so though, be mindful of your body—especially as it ages. At the time of writing, I am a few months into dealing with a pinched nerve. At one point, I couldn't lift my right arm above my shoulder. The culprit was a behind-the-neck weightlifting exercise I never should've been doing in the first place. See, five years ago, after discovering herniations in my cervical spine, my doctor told me never to lift over my head again. Acknowledge your changing limits with grace. It'll save you a lot of pain.

As you develop your routines, it's important to plan for the long haul.

In my case, dropping 30 pounds to get to 220 will take stress off my back, neck, and knees, as well as improving the speed my body recovers at. That means more physical therapy, more stretching, and more functional training. It means laying off the weights and letting go of some ego.

A big motivator is my kids. I had them later in life, so when they're in the prime of their teenage years, I'll be pushing 60. I want to keep up with them. That means training smart. I work with trainers, and I recommend everyone do the same if they can. Having more than one gym helps too—it keeps you from getting complacent or turning your workout into a social hour. And don't skip flexibility work: Yoga, stretching, and mobility drills, especially as you get older, can make a huge difference in your outcomes.

I've also trained with partners, and the right one will push you harder than you'll push yourself.

The best experience I ever had was when I started working with a professional health coach and bodybuilder. Someone who lives this lifestyle on every level to this day with no signs of slowing down. He wasn't just a coach, he was an international champion in both bodybuilding and powerlifting, with a Bachelor's Degree in Sports Science and Master's Degree in Sports Nutrition. He came from a culture where physical strength and discipline were deeply ingrained—rooted in the legacy of the former Soviet Union, where being strong wasn't just about looks, it was a matter of national pride and mental toughness. This meant his approach wasn't just about lifting weights or eating clean, it was about building identity, understanding biology, and aligning every part of your life with nature and in light of the person you wanted to become.

We trained, ate, and lived like bodybuilders. It was exhausting and time-consuming, but very eye-opening. I ate more than I ever had in my life, didn't gain a pound, and put on muscle while burning fat. The lesson? If you want to see what's possible, put yourself next to someone who lives that life. The accountability, structure, and knowledge they can offer are game changers.

Of course, training is only half the battle. Meal prep matters too. But you have to be realistic and create habits that you can stick to. For the average person, the simplest rule is to eat every three hours: a portion of clean protein about the size of your fist, plus a healthy starch like white rice, sweet potatoes, or oatmeal. Keep each meal in the 350–450 calorie range. This means eating five to six small meals a day, which is tough for many people to pull off, so I like the "meal-shake-meal-shake" method. You alternate between a meal and then a shake and then a meal and so on. It's not perfect—your body absorbs whole, unprocessed foods better—but it's a lot better than skipping meals or grabbing junk. The focus should be on protein. The truth is that most people just do not get enough. We are inundated with carb heavy foods and processed sugary

EVERYTHING. From pumpkin spiced this to vanilla or caramel that. Adopt the general rule of thumb that when it comes to food, if it wasn't around 2,000 years ago, it's probably not good for you.

Post-workout, whey protein and a fast-digesting carb like a banana help with recovery. But make sure to get this in your body within 30 minutes after working out. Before workouts, some carbs, like oatmeal with honey, can give you the fuel to push harder. But wait at least 45 minutes before working out after eating. The biggest myth I've busted is that carbs are the enemy. When I trained with the bodybuilder, I ate more carbs than ever and still leaned out. The key is using them *intelligently*.

Another oft overlooked health hack. Go for a simple 10-15 minute walk immediately after eating to help boost your insulin sensitivity. Insulin sensitivity is your body's ability to effectively use insulin to move glucose from the blood into your cells for energy. Simply put, if you eat and then plop yourself down on the couch, there is no need for energy use and so your body will move into calorie storage mode. Get into the habit of going for a post meal walk, however, and your body will eventually learn to immediately start using those calories for energy instead of storing them and eventually leading to weight gain amongst other health issues. This can be measured using a simple "fat loss panel" style blood test. Unfortunately, this isn't something your hospital-based medical provider will offer. So, you're going to have to seek these out on your own. I promise it's worth it.

But remember you can't just go hard Monday through Friday and blow it all on the weekend. That's the fastest way to stall progress. Getting in shape is a long game, made up of small, hard-to-notice wins spread out over time. That's why it's wrapped up with identity. Who you think you are shapes your lifestyle in profound ways. Make yourself a person who gets a little movement in every day and cares what you put in your body.

My coach, Juris Skribans, was kind enough to put together a list of "daily habits for health reinvention" for this chapter. With 20 years of experience, Juris knows a thing or two about helping people live happier, healthier, and stronger:

"It's one thing to read about transformation—it's another to live it. This appendix was created to help you do exactly that. As someone who's worked behind the scenes with the author on his health journey, I've seen firsthand how identity, habits, and biology all intersect. Lasting change doesn't come from willpower alone—it comes from choosing, day after day, to act in alignment with who you want to become.

This habit sheet and checklist aren't just about losing weight or looking better—they're about building a system for becoming the strongest, most capable version of yourself. The one who moves with energy, thinks clearly, sleeps deeply, and lives with purpose. Use this appendix as your daily compass. Mark the boxes. Reflect on the prompts. Build momentum one step at a time. You don't need perfection—just consistency and ownership. If you want health to become your new identity, this is where it begins."

| Category | Habit | Notes |
| --- | --- | --- |
| Morning Light & Movement | 10–20 min walk outside before 10am | Syncs circadian rhythm, boosts dopamine |
| Hydration & Electrolytes | 1L water with pinch of sea salt & lemon upon waking | Supports energy, digestion, and blood pressure |
| First Meal of the Day | Protein + fats + whole foods only | Avoid carbs early to stay in fat-burning zone and retain mental clarity (unless training early) |
| Sunlight Exposure | 15–30 min midday sun on skin/eyes (no sunglasses) | Critical for serotonin & vitamin D synthesis |
| Aerobic Training | 20–30 min zone 2 cardio (bike, walk, swim) 3x/week | Improves metabolic flexibility, fat oxidation, deuterium depletion |
| Strength Training | 2–4x/week depending on goal | Focus on compound lifts or functional bodyweight training |
| Mindset Rewire | 5–10 min journaling or self-identity work | Affirm the new identity: "I am becoming the person I admire" |
| Meal Timing | Focus on eating only during daylight hours (no snacking at night) | Leverages circadian biology for hormone health |
| Evening Ritual | Screens off by 8pm, dim lights, no food 3 hrs before bed | Supports melatonin and deep recovery |
| Cold or Heat Exposure | 2–10 min cold shower or sauna 3–4x/week, especially effective after training if recovery is the primary goal | Stimulates mitochondria & hormone resilience |

# Identity Check-In (Daily Mindset Prompts)

1. Who am I choosing to become today?

2. Are my actions aligned with the future I want to live in?

3. What excuse am I ready to stop telling myself?

4. Where can I find a small win right now?

## In Summary:

- Lasting change starts with shifting how you see yourself, not just what you eat or how you exercise.

- Understand why you eat the way you do and focus on sustainable, long-term habits over quick results.

- Nutrition, movement, environment, media, and self-image all shape your overall well-being.

- Adapt workouts to your body's needs, use accountability partners, and prioritize flexibility and injury prevention.

- Moderate indulgence, balanced nutrition, and daily movement create progress you can maintain.

# 8

# ENERGY

## The Energy You Carry

When we talk about energy, people often picture something mystical or abstract; that what you put out is what you get back. But the truth is simpler: the energy you bring into the world has a way of manifesting itself in your life. If you put your best out there, you'll be amazed by what returns.

Looking back, I can see that the earliest energy I received came from my mother. She poured love, patience, and encouragement into me at a cellular level. Scientists will tell you that the chemistry of a mother's body during pregnancy—her stress levels, her calm, her presence—can shape a child more than we realize. We spend our whole lives, from the womb onward, absorbing frequencies from the people around us.

Energy has a profound effect in shaping the lens through which we see the world. These manifestations are probably the reason why like seems to so consistently attract like. A person who's constantly sick with worry often gets sick in reality. A person who carries generosity usually finds it returned to them.

My mother embodied that principle. She was and *is* generous; to a fault. She's always looking for the good and always believing the best in people; something I picked up from her. Just recently, a repairman came to her condo to patch up the air conditioner. After some time on the roof he explained that the A/C problem involved a big fix and would eventually require that the unit be replaced, which was something he didn't do. He loaded her up with freon, to buy her some more time with the existing A/C unit. He didn't really solve the long term problem, and only charged $150 for the patch job. She still tipped him fifty dollars.

But then my mother was always generous with her time and affections. She took care of people in the neighborhood all my life, providing meals and shelter to kids in need. Even when I see it as too much, I love and appreciate the spirit she carries, and what it taught me about being a better person.

But the reverse can also be true. We sometimes become more like the people we resist. I've seen family members who spent years fighting against the influence of a parent only to end up mirroring the same bitterness and energy they hated. That's the double edged nature of energy. It doesn't just pass through us, it leaves an imprint.

So as you pass through life remember, knowingly or unknowingly, we are always absorbing and projecting energy. It shapes who we become, it shapes what comes back to us, and it shapes the people we interact with.

# Energy in Relationships

Trust is one of those words that people define in very different ways. But in general, we tend to trust people who align with the rhythms of our own energy. Moreover, successful relationships are going to be built not just on trust, but on exchange; on a certain reciprocity of energy.

In any relationship, there are times when we give and times when we take; the balance is almost never 50/50. Picture a battery with a full charge. If two people are drawing on that same battery, one might be using 85% of it at a given moment, while the other is left with 15%. The roles can reverse depending on the day, but the balance is rarely even.

I see this in my own marriage. Most of the time, we're each focused on different things and because of this, we're carrying different weights. But every so often, we line up perfectly. Recently, we worked together setting up a lemonade stand for our daughter. It was one of the rare times we were in

complete synchronicity—squeezing lemons, mix-
ing the batch, running the assembly line. There
was no give-or-take struggle, just a shared goal and
a shared flow.

That's the exception, though. Most of the time,
relationships are a dance of energy exchange. One
person is listening while the other is venting. One
is carrying the load while the other is handing
it off. We have to be careful though: when that
exchange gets too far out of balance, resentment
creeps in.

And it's not just marriages. Children are a constant draw on energy. They give back in flash-
es—an "I love you," a good report from school, a
random hug—but most of the time, they're tak-
ers. That's not a flaw; it's just the way life works.
Children don't come into the world to fill your
cup; they come needing you to fill theirs.

The challenge is being aware of that dance, because if you're not, you wake up one day feeling
completely depleted without even realizing how

you got that way. Energy in relationships isn't just about love or duty, it's about reciprocity. And if reciprocity is missing, the battery eventually dies. It's important to try and be conscious of these exchanges so that you can show up as your best self.

## When Energy Turns Toxic

Not all energy we project is good energy. I've been on both sides of that truth.

Just the other day I cut someone off in traffic without meaning to. The guy was furious. He started honking, trying to chase me down, and eventually swerved in front of me like he was trying to win some personal war with me. Years ago, I would have met that energy head-on. Years ago, I was that guy. It would have turned into a whole showdown. But this time I just laughed. Not because I was better than him, but because I recognized myself in him. That was me, years ago—angry, full of blame, and ready to escalate over nothing.

The only reason I didn't bite this time was because I had better energy with me. My wife was in the car, and we were celebrating the fact that she'd just had a successful surgery. We were thinking about creating a new life and were pretty far removed from the petty concerns of roadway politics.

But I wasn't always like that. In my twenties, I carried blame like it was oxygen. I brought it into first dates, into conversations, into every room I entered. And a lot of people felt it. My wife still jokes about how angry I seemed when we first met. The truth is, that anger was real. I was frustrated with life, my perceptions of unfairness, and the cards I'd been dealt. Left unchecked, that energy eventually landed me in prison.

It took a while, but eventually I learned that anger is poison. Without an outlet, it spills over—sometimes outward into aggression, sometimes inward into depression. Turned inward, anger eats you alive. Turned outward, it wrecks your relationships, your future, and takes away your freedom. I've lived on both sides of that.

And here's the hard truth: anger is something we all struggle with. Young men in particular: testosterone, frustration, the desire to prove yourself...all this can leave you with a huge chip on your shoulder. Without role models or healthy outlets, that chip becomes dangerous. Some boys find sports, some find mentors, and some are lucky enough to have fathers or coaches to guide them. Others don't, and they end up carrying that chip until it breaks them.

I've interviewed people who found their role models in unexpected places—on TV, in books, through school and a hundred other places besides. And we should be open to that. I think that we're wired to look for someone a little further down the path to show us the ropes. Even my own son shadows older kids, copying everything they do. That's human nature: we learn by watching, imitating, absorbing energy from the people around us.

But the energy you absorb is the energy you become. That's why finding people that help get the chip off your shoulder is so important. For me, fulfillment became the cure. You don't manage road rage by white-knuckling the wheel. You manage it by being at peace with your life, so the little stuff doesn't trigger you anymore.

I had to learn the hard way. At one point, my philosophy was "an eye for an eye." If someone wronged me, I'd hit back harder. That mentality got me into fights, got me locked up, and got me tossed into solitary. I remember a counselor in prison pointing out the obvious pattern: "Someone wronged you, so you hurt them. Someone stole from you, so you wanted to hurt them. That's why you're here. Apparently, you have not learned your lesson yet, Mr. Martin." It hit me like a slap. Needless to say, I was livid.

They weren't wrong though.

That's the cost of toxic energy: you think you're winning the exchange, but really, you're just burning yourself down. Like Gandhi said, "An eye for an eye makes the whole world blind."

## Energy in Business

The same laws of energy that govern romantic and family relationships also govern your business relationships. In the early days, when you're just starting out, hunger drives you. Especially with your first venture. If you're doing it right, you're all in. You could be out on the road four days a week, wake up thinking about the business, and go to bed thinking about it. Every thought, every ounce of focus goes into building. But you've only got one battery, and if 80% of it is going into the business, that means your family isn't getting enough, your spouse isn't getting enough, and your health isn't getting enough. Something always suffers.

That's why I say balance is a myth. At least if by "balance" you mean a steady state. Life never stays level. It's like a heartbeat monitor. It moves up and down, always passing through spikes and dips. When you run a business, it can sometimes take almost everything. Later, when you find success or bring on the right help, you can reclaim some of that energy and put it back into health, family, or whatever else you've been neglecting. But in the building stage? Forget balance. You're just riding the line and trying not to fall off.

Even the biggest names don't escape it. You'll never convince me that someone like Elon Musk isn't sacrificing his relationship with his kids in the process of chasing his ventures. He's an example of what imbalance looks like at the extreme. But how many hard working fathers and mothers are inadvertently neglecting their roles as parents in pursuit of their worldly ambitions? I'm not judging because I've done it too. But instead of balance consider work/life integration. More or less, you can be more intentional with your time and make sure to include the children and your significant other. Try scheduling your work around your family instead of doing what most of us do, which is the exact opposite. Especially entrepreneurs.

For me, the lesson really came home when I hit a patch of legal trouble. I had two lawsuits going at the same time. One started in March and dragged on for more than a year. The other started in August and was wrapped up by the end of the year. The difference wasn't the outcome—both ended more or less the same way. The difference was the energy I put into them.

With the long case, every call from the lawyer set me off. I'd hang up and stew over how unfair the system was, why the whole thing was ridiculous. It took me emotionally high and then dropped me into anger and frustration. But eventually I learned to let it go. Once I accepted that it was in my attorney's hands, it was out of mine. All the energy I was pouring into it could be redirected in more productive ways. Remember: it's okay to be upset or angry. Just make sure you get it out in a healthy way. Then move on.

And that's the point. Other people let lawsuits like that drain the life out of them—they're on the phone with their lawyers every few days, chasing progress when the next hearing isn't even scheduled for a month. All that's just energy wasted. It's a common mistake we make in business to fixate on what's outside our control.

Years ago, if I'd still been drinking, I wouldn't have had the clarity to handle my situations. I'd have spun myself out completely. But sobriety gave me a lot of clarity around energy management. Pour yourself into the things you can control. Learn to identify the things you can't. And don't waste your battery on the battles that won't change no matter how much juice you give them.

That's what Reinhold Niebuhr's Serenity Prayer is really about. It's not just a mantra you repeat. It's an energy management strategy:

> *"God, grant me the serenity to accept the things I cannot change, courage to change the things I can, and wisdom to know the difference."*

Entrepreneurship always begins with a kind of faith. Faith starts with an almost naive belief that you can bend the world to your will if you just work hard enough. In the early stages, that faith often shows up as control. You're solving problems on the fly, building the business, and attempting to force outcomes by sheer determination. It's one manifestation of what psychologists call fluid intelligence: the ability to improvise, adapt, and push through with raw problem-solving power.

But the real wisdom comes later. Arthur Brooks, a Harvard professor, talks about how high achievers transition from fluid intelligence to something called crystallized intelligence. That's when you stop trying to control everything and allow your prior knowledge and experience to guide your actions. You recognize that the steps themselves rather than your grip on the outcome are what move you forward. The happiest people are the ones who make that shift gracefully.

The ones who don't? They often spiral into the classic midlife crisis. C'mon, you've seen those guys at the Vegas pool parties and nightclubs.

Not knowing when to hang it up. They cling to control, but the world doesn't bend anymore. So, they spend or distract themselves. They buy sports cars, blow money on wild trips, or numb out with golf and booze. It's not that they've lost the capacity for success; it's that they've refused to evolve. Instead of creating something more meaningful or legacy-driven, they double down on their own unmet expectations.

The shift from control to faith doesn't just happen once in a lifetime. It's a process that unfolds through every business, every project, and every cycle of building a life. At first, you're in startup mode: improvising, hustling, and holding everything together with your bare hands. But if you stay in that mode too long, you burn out. To keep going, you have to learn to let go, to trust the systems you've built, and to move from being the operator to being the guide.

That's the deeper transition: the move from that follows mastery is into the role of teacher.

# The Law of Hypnotic Rhythm

Napoleon Hill had this idea he called the Law of Hypnotic Rhythm. It boils down to this: do something long enough and it becomes a groove, one that can be exceptionally hard to get out of. It's like your personal autopilot; a rhythm that either drags you down or carries you forward.

Habits are funny that way. As I said before, they can be the best of servants or the worst of masters. When you're in the wrong rhythm, especially when you don't even realize it, you just get stuck in a loop, caught in the matrix, and doing the same dumb shit over and over.

And energy? Energy is the gasoline powering that motor. Like so much of where I came from; low-rent energy—stealing, lying, drinking, numbing yourself, doing whatever you can just to survive—locks you into a low-rent rhythm. You're operating at the basement frequency, syncing up with negativity, and before long you don't even notice it's who you are. High-rent energy—gratitude, kindness, contribution—that's when you start riding a different wave. And once you're conscious of it, once you can stop yourself mid-loop and jump tracks, life gets a whole lot easier. It's like momentum finally kicks in, and life starts working for you instead of against you.

I know, because I've lived on both sides. For years I filled my tank with garbage fuel—food, women, gambling, drugs, and alcohol. All of it just kept me sputtering along, my engine never running clean. Alcohol was the worst of it. Booze lowered my inhibitions just enough to get me doing things my aware self would never touch. But it was comfortable, and comfort is a hell of a drug. So I stayed in that rhythm, riding wave after wave of self-destruction like it was the only current available.

The truth? I was hypnotized. Locked in a rhythm I didn't even know I was dancing to.

But here's the good news: rhythms can be broken. This year I celebrated three years sober. Quitting drinking wasn't just about cutting alcohol; it was about jacking myself out of that old rhythm and tuning into a higher frequency. In other words, three years ago, I snapped out of the trance.

What hypnotic rhythm are you caught in? What has you stuck on autopilot and heading in the wrong direction? Are you holding on to a toxic relationship you know you need to leave? Does your marriage feel dead? Are you miserable at a job you hate? Drinking to excess? Eating too much? What is just one thing that you know you can eliminate and your life will be instantly better for it?

So, start being mindful of your hypnotic rhythms. Mastering it is the difference between a slow death trapped in the same low-rent cycles or finding the rocket fuel that takes you some place better.

## The Aware Self

There's the version of me that knows better—I call it the *aware self*. And then there's the me that defaults to old habits and patterns. The aware self knows the right moves. It knows to hit the gym, skip the drink, and to wake up clear-headed. But the old me? He reached for distractions. He'll tell himself, "I had a rough day; I need to process; let's have a few drinks; or get high today." That's the negative hypnotic rhythm coming out. It wasn't even about the weed. It. was about procrastination dressed up as self-care.

If you listen to your aware self, you can get these things under control. That's where the tools come in. Focus on meditation, breathwork, staying grounded, and getting exercise. Maybe all the talk about vibrational frequencies sounds a little woo-woo, but I assure you there's something to it. If you ditch your phone and take a walk in nature, you feel better. As always, the secret sauce is simple; take some kind of ACTION to break the old patterns of behavior.

On the flip side, there are hypnotic rhythms I've *chosen* that serve me. The gym is the biggest one. It's non-negotiable now, just a flow I fall into. In fact, I don't remember the last time I went a week without getting in some kind of intentional movement, whether it be walking, stretching, push-ups, or something. Fitness is a guardrail, keeping me aligned with my aware self.

Family obligations help too. These days, even if I fall off track, I bounce back faster because I've got accountability. My family, my wife, and my kids notice when I'm out of alignment. And that awareness brings me back to center a whole lot quicker.

## Be The Light

When it's all said and done, the energy I want to put into the world is simple: I want to be the light. I want to be the guy I needed when I was down and out. I want to be a mentor that someone else can lean on. I want to plant seeds of hope, gratitude, compassion, and understanding. Call it what you want, but at the core, it's built from love.

At a Tony Robbins *Date with Destiny* seminar, I actually wrote down the purpose of my life. It wasn't flashy or complicated—it was this:

> *"I will be a vessel of grace and kindness; enjoy the little things God blesses me with, and to do good deeds for myself and others."*

That's it. That's what became my north star.

From there, I broke my purpose into five pillars: love, faith, health, contribution, and peace.

- Anytime I'm kind towards another human being, anytime I look my family in the eyes and tell them I love them, anytime I hug someone that needs it, anytime I listen to a viewpoint that I don't agree with, anytime I truly listen to someone with intent, I'm being LOVE.

- When I start my day with prayer, work with humility and patience in the moment, admit that I don't have the answers and it's okay, or see the presence of God in the little things, or step into appreciation, I am in FAITH.

- The times I exercise or drink water. Anytime I learn something new about health and fitness. Anytime I eat something natural, nutritious. Anytime I meditate or take a deep breath. Anytime I drink a protein shake, I'm contributing to my HEALTH.

- CONTRIBUTION is giving without expecting, whether it's time, money, or just a meaningful conversation with another human being.

- And PEACE—peace is the hardest and the most important. For me, peace is prayer. It's meditation. It's sitting in nature with no phone in my hand.

So, yeah, I'll say it plain: I believe in God, and I believe in magic. And I also know all these things come down to me—how I show up, what energy I put out, what rhythm I choose to dance to. And if I can be intentional with my energy, then maybe I really can be the light for somebody else.

## In Summary

- The frequencies we project—love, anger, generosity, bitterness—don't just affect others, they shape what comes back to us.

- Whether in marriage, parenting, or business, energy exchange is rarely 50/50, but awareness of the balance prevents resentment and burnout.

- Anger and blame can imprison you—literally and figuratively—while fulfillment, purpose, and role models help redirect that charge into something positive.

- Early entrepreneurship runs on raw hustle, but long-term success depends on shifting from control to trust, from operator to teacher.

- Habits and "hypnotic rhythms" either trap you in cycles of destruction or carry you into growth; being intentional about your energy lets you write a better groove.

# 9

# LOVE AND GRATITUDE—THE HEART OF PURPOSE

## Love as Purpose

I owe everything I am today to love.

Love has been the foundation of my growth, my success, and it sits at the very heart of my sense of purpose. My mother instilled love in me early and often through my childhood, teenage years, and even as a young adult navigating life. Despite her own struggles, she never let them harden her heart.

Instead, she led with compassion, generosity, and an unwavering belief in helping others.

Love, in the "unconditional" sense, is selfless. It puts others before oneself. It does not judge, expect, or resent. Yet, as I've grown, I've realized that this kind of love is difficult to embody. As relationships mature, we naturally develop expectations around them. When those expectations aren't met, we can feel disappointed, resentful, or like things are out of balance—like we give more than we receive (or vice versa). But love isn't really transactional like that. It lives beyond reciprocity; it is a gift we offer freely.

Keeping score will ultimately lead to nothing good. Instead, simply trade your expectations for appreciation. I know it's easier said than done—but let's give it a try.

Here's what I mean. When I was younger, I once felt frustrated with a close friend who never seemed to match the energy I put into our relationship. I carried that resentment like a stone in my chest until, one day, I decided to stop measuring the friendship. I asked myself instead, *what do I appreciate about this person?* The answer came quickly: they made me laugh when I was down, they showed up in moments that mattered, they accepted me as I was. Once I shifted from expecting more to appreciating what was there, the weight lifted. Our relationship improved—not because they changed, but because I rid myself of expectations and simply focused on appreciating their presence. I use this technique in my marriage all the time. If you start keeping score, everyone loses.

Love is the greatest power we have. It's the force that can change the world. Those who have love in their lives always have something to return to, something that anchors them through hardship. Without it, people face loneliness, hopelessness, and despair. When love is absent, people can be far more susceptible to seeking belonging in the wrong environments.

# Love and Compassion

Practicing love starts by practicing compassion. Again, growing up I was blessed: my mother had a big heart, and I like to think her example helped me grow mine. The most valuable lesson she ever taught me was how to care for others, to never look down on people, and to put myself in their shoes.

My mother embodied this truth. She was a woman who would give you her last five dollars if you needed to eat. Her home was a sanctuary for those in need—whether it was a family member freshly out of jail with nowhere to go, or a cousin recently kicked out of their house. Our home became a refuge.

She was a social worker by trade, dedicating her entire career to serving others. Early on, she worked in special education but found it too painful to watch the system fail children with disabilities. So she transitioned to social work, specifically in welfare services for the City of New York.

Many of her colleagues treated their jobs as burdens, ignoring calls and looking down on those seeking help. My mother was different. She embraced people with kindness and respect, earning the love and gratitude of the same people society had dismissed. Her clients brought her gifts, homemade food, and heartfelt cards of appreciation. She gave so much of herself to the people she served.

Later, she took on an even greater challenge—working with people battling HIV/AIDS. At the time, HIV/AIDS patients were among the most marginalized in society, abandoned out of fear and ignorance. She often had to enter dangerous neighborhoods to reach them, but she never hesitated. And by the grace of God, she was always safe. I believe He protected her because her heart was pure. God is love, and love is a force that shields those who walk in its light.

Her example taught me this: love is the opposite of fear. Fear breeds doubt, uncertainty, and hesitation. It's love that allows us to break free from these chains. Love is understanding, non-judgmental, and unconditional. When we embrace love, we liberate ourselves from the mental and emotional prisons we've built. Fear falls away when you fully step into love. But this wasn't something I grasped immediately. Life had to teach me in the only way I was going to listen: the hard way.

## Love Saves

At 29, I found myself at the beginning of my two-year prison sentence. It could have been the darkest period of my life—but it wasn't, because love was there. My now-wife, Jennifer, had come into my life a year before I turned myself in. Our first anniversary was just two days after I walked into that prison.

Her love gave me hope. It gave me purpose. Without Jennifer's letters—without the knowledge that someone was waiting for me—my prison experience would have been entirely different. Because of her, instead of despair, I found clarity.

Instead of bitterness, I found ambition. I spent those two years setting goals, dreaming big, and writing down my vision for the future. If I had been alone, I don't know where I would be today. But because I had love, I had something to fight for and to come home to. Today, I can clearly say that my wife helped save my life. Neither of us knew it back then, but God put us in each other's lives to give us both purpose

This is why I believe love is the reason for everything. It's the reason I am here. It's the reason you're reading this book. It's the reason we step into our purpose. God's love has carried each of us through struggles we thought we wouldn't survive. That nagging feeling in your heart—the one urging you toward something greater—that's love guiding you to your purpose.

Love is an energy, a frequency. The universe operates on vibrations, and I believe the heart emits its own. My mother's heart resonated at a wavelength of compassion, and she was guided and protected because of it. When you lead with love, you attract love. Good people, opportunities, and blessings find their way to you. I've tried to carry on my mother's vibration in my own life.

## We Have to Believe in Something

I was raised Catholic, a result of my Dominican heritage. While church wasn't the center of our life, we did go almost weekly to a local parish. I did my first communion but never returned to Sunday school after that. My mother's explanation for religion was simple: *"We have to believe in something. We have to have rules or people will do whatever they want."*

For a long time, that didn't stick. Through my late teens and twenties, I drifted far from faith. I lived as an atheist, believing only in my ability to make things happen. Sure, I was making things happen—but my life was a mess. Aimless, selfish, numbing myself with parties, drinking, and drugs. There were fun times, no doubt, but nothing lasting came of it. It was just empty debauchery. In hindsight, I realize those years taught me a lot about who Sean *wasn't*.

So I decided to get sober, and that changed everything. Once I got clean, I started to feel something stirring in me again. I prayed—not because I thought God owed me anything, but because I finally recognized my need for guidance. Slowly, my relationship with God grew deeper. Prayer became how I aligned myself with purpose. Every morning, I asked for strength, for clarity, and for opportunities to serve. I thanked Him for both blessings and more importantly, for the struggles, because both had shaped me into the man I am.

My faith has given me the strength to be a better husband, father, son, friend, and leader. Love, purpose, and faith are not separate forces—they are intertwined. Love fuels our mission, faith sustains us, and purpose gives our lives meaning. When we align these forces, we unlock a power greater than ourselves. We become unstoppable.

## Gratitude as Practice

If love is the foundation, gratitude is the daily practice. There is no more powerful yet simple way to change one's life than by being thankful. Gratitude is a perspective shift—a new way of seeing the world that can transform even the most difficult moments into opportunities for growth.

To practice gratitude, we focus on what we have rather than what we lack. Even in moments of struggle or misfortune, gratitude has the power to change everything. Gratitude challenges our worldview: instead of "life is unfair, the world is against me," we say, "life is teaching me, the world is shaping me."

This doesn't mean ignoring pain. Some events are brutal—abuse, trauma, and tragedy. But while we may not control what happens, we can control how we respond. That response determines whether we remain trapped in the past or move forward with resilience. It is a simple but monumental shift away from asking, *"Why me?"* to asking, *"What is this teaching me?"*

I once met a man who had lost his teenage son in a school shooting. The grief nearly destroyed him. But instead of being consumed by bitterness, he and his wife started a foundation in their son's name. They now provide scholarships to young people pursuing education in peace and conflict resolution. Their tragedy did not vanish—it never could—but gratitude gave them a way to transform pain into purpose.

Another close friend of mine lost her husband to a heart attack. He was a firefighter and ex-military veteran. Her faith in Christ and search for meaning in his sudden passing led her to form a foundation that brings together the widows and families of fallen firefighters, police officers and military veterans. Simply stated, she had the courage to turn her pain into purpose and serve something greater than herself.

## Gratitude, Empathy, and Grace

Compassion and empathy are blessings that gratitude cultivates. Many people are their own harshest critics, punishing themselves with endless loops of self-blame. *"I should have known better. I always mess things up. I'm not enough."* That inner dialogue can become a prison, trapping us in shame and regret. Gratitude interrupts that cycle.

When we practice gratitude for who we are and what we've survived, we soften toward ourselves. We stop focusing only on the scars and start honoring the fact that we made it through battles others may never even see. That shift matters, because when you can extend grace inward, you naturally begin to extend it outward. Self-compassion opens the door for compassion toward others.

Empathy grows from that place. It allows us to stop dwelling on unfairness and instead focus on possibility. Instead of *"Why me?"* we begin to ask, *"What can I do with what I have?"* That simple change in perspective can transform a victim mindset into a builder's mindset. Gratitude gives us the courage to say: *Yes, life has been hard. But look at what it has given me: perspective, resilience, and endurance. Now how can I use these?*

When leadership, relationships, and daily interactions are guided by empathy, life becomes richer and more meaningful. Imagine a workplace where managers lead with gratitude—where employees are seen not just as workers but as people with lives, challenges, and talents worth recognizing. Imagine a family where each member pauses to give thanks for one another, even in conflict. Those aren't just nice ideas; they are shifts in culture that ripple outward. Gratitude creates compassion. Compassion fuels empathy. And empathy changes the way we move through the world, one interaction at a time.

## Gratitude as a Life Hack

Life has never been fair, and it likely never will be. Inequity exists everywhere. But how we choose to see it shapes our experience. Consider: most of the world lives on less than two dollars a day—less than the average American spends on a cup of coffee. That fact can make us cynical, or it can make us grateful for opportunities we might otherwise take for granted.

Practicing gratitude doesn't require grand gestures. It can be as simple as:

- Offering a kind word to a stranger.

- Saying good morning to someone who looks down.

- Thanking the waiter who refills your water.

- Smiling at the barista who serves you coffee.

Small acts of gratitude make the world kinder. They remind us that no matter our struggles, we are connected, and we have something to give.

## In Summary

- Love and gratitude are not abstract ideals; they are daily choices. Love is the force that defeats fear. Gratitude is the practice that reshapes struggle into strength.

- Love is the driving force behind personal growth—not just an emotion but a guiding principle.

- Gratitude is the lens that turns hardship into wisdom. When combined, they give us clarity, resilience, and a foundation to build lives of meaning.

- When you lead with love and live in gratitude, you attract goodness. And you discover, as I have, that the heart of everything—every success, every blessing, every struggle survived—is love.

# CONCLUSION

## Looking Back, Looking Forward

When you sit down and start pulling the threads of your life together, you begin to see the puzzle from a distance. Patterns emerge that you didn't notice before. Fleeting moments that seemed small at the time suddenly take on weight. And you realize that it's not always the dramatic "*aha*" events that define you. Instead, it's the accumulation of little things; the words spoken before or after, the decisions made in passing, that ultimately led us to the paths we followed.

I think back to those long nights in prison, sitting on a steel bunk with nothing but a notebook and a pen. But slowly I realized I was rebuilding myself, line by line. The words I wrote back then showed me something about who I was and who I wanted to be. Prison gave me the space to decide I was never going back—to those walls, or to the man I'd been before them. And I suppose my life couldn't really begin until I'd figured that out.

So writing this book has been eye-opening for me. It's provided me a chance to zoom out, take a bird's-eye view of my own story, and to see myself with a new kind of clarity. Some of what I saw has been humbling. I was reminded of how valuable even the mistakes were, and I could laugh at just how ridiculous some of my early attempts at success were.

I was also able to expand my perspective. Exploring my story and seeing it written on the page allowed me to confront things I hadn't seen clearly before. Like anyone, I wanted to cast myself as the hero of my own story. And heroes, by definition, can't always see their own flaws. Putting the words down made me face them.

For example, I once dismissed the idea that men could struggle with issues of physical appearance in the same way women do. That was a wake-up call when I realized how much of my own identity had been tied up in body image over the years. Another example was my time in prison. I'd always wrestled with how much of that story belonged here. For a long time I wanted to shrink it down, hide it, pretend it was less impactful than it really was. But seeing it written out, as one chapter among many, gave me a healthier perspective: it was part of my life, yes, but just a part. It wasn't the whole story, and it didn't need to dominate the narrative.

Even the act of writing this book proved the point. There were moments I stalled, thinking, *The story's not finished. I can't write this until I've figured it all out.* But the truth is, we never figure it all out. The lessons will keep coming. And even in writing these chapters, new lessons surfaced. That was one of the surprises: the process itself taught me as much as the life it hoped to describe.

# Why This Book

I'd love to say I wrote this book for all the right reasons. The truth is a project like this demands a lot of ego. For years, whenever I'd tell my story, people would tell me, "You've lived an interesting life—you should write a book." And for more than a decade, I carried that idea around. "Someday," I said.

But the real push came later when I started seeing some important shifts in my industry. I knew I needed a pivot, so I asked myself what I really wanted to do with my time and energy. And it wasn't hard to figure out: I wanted to inspire people. I wanted to connect, to share the lessons I'd learned, and to use my voice and my gifts for something bigger. And looking back, this seed was planted in me while I was writing in those black and white notebooks while locked up.

*"I will have a career giving back and teaching others to reach for their*

*dreams; teaching them the tools to do it while making a living that provided an eight-figure income"*
-Sean Martin
*Note from prison, July, 9, 2010*

I know that this book will play an important part in getting me started on that journey. At first, it was an exercise, something I did in order to prove to myself that I could. But as I wrote, it also became therapy. It was like putting the puzzle of my life together for the first time and connecting so many dots. Seeing my life through the eyes of my editor also helped me to put things into perspective in ways that I had previously overlooked.

And it takes a little ego to think that you could be a mentor to others. Not really having one as I grew up meant that I had to stumble through mistakes that could have been avoided. And while I wouldn't change the journey, I now feel called to be the kind of example I wish I'd had. To young men and women growing up in circumstances like mine, you are loved, you are capable, and you are not bound by your circumstances.

This book is for them—but it's not only for them. It's also for those who have already "made it," but who still feel empty. I've seen too many people who've checked every box, be they career, money, or possessions, and still wonder what it's all for. A meaningful life isn't just about getting more money. A meaningful life is made so by what we give back to our communities, our children, and to our collective future. Because giving is living.

And giving doesn't always mean writing a check. The most valuable thing you can share is your knowledge, your story, and your time. I've never seen someone open up about their struggles and not come away feeling lighter, freer, and more purposeful. We're meant to pay it forward. That's why cultures across the world honor the wisdom of their elders—why the teachings in every holy book echo the same lessons of compassion, resilience, and love. The tools aren't new. But they do need to be passed on.

That's what I want this book to do: to take the lessons of a life lived—hard lessons, painful lessons, beautiful lessons—and pass them forward. It's a record of where I've been and what I've learned. But more than that, it's a bridge. connecting me to those who might benefit from my example and connecting them to each other.

This book has also connected me more deeply to my own family. When my wife read the first few chapters, she texted me: "Reminds me of the reasons I fell in love with you... You're a badass, but also a very loving and compassionate person who wears his heart on his sleeve. I love you so much. We've survived through a lot."

She also told me that after reading about how I was already walking to school and going to the store alone at eight years old, she sent our daughter in to buy bread and peanut butter by herself; a small step toward independence.

So I've decided to let some of those concerns about ego go. It's okay to have a little ego drive your work if your aims are noble. Maybe that how we get some emotional skin in the game—its okay to feel good about wanting to do good.

## Perspective and Progress

If I could go back and speak to my younger self, before the prison years, before the weight of so many choices, I'd tell him a few simple things. *It's okay not to have all the answers. It's okay to feel anger, but don't let anger control you. Remember that anger is often just fear and insecurity wearing a mask. Be patient—life really is a marathon, not a sprint.*

Some of these lessons only became clear much later. I think of my father, who was absent for most of my life. A few years ago, he passed away. Growing up, I'd spent very little time with him, and it wasn't until the end that we had a handful of moments together. I remember one in particular: my daughter's baby shower. He showed up frail, in his eighties, and leaning on a cane. But a couple glasses of Johnny Walker Blue, and suddenly he was light on his feet again—dancing with the women and charming the room. At that moment, as we were welcoming new life, I got to see the man who helped create mine.

He and my mother, who hadn't spoken in more than thirty years, got to converse and reconnect. He told her that she'd done a great job with me, and maybe that was something I had always needed to hear. I hadn't realized until much later how important a father's presence—or absence—can be. My mother gave me love, strength, and compassion in abundance, but she couldn't teach me how to be a man. That kind of guidance had to come from somewhere else. A boy needs that influence from a male figure in their life, and I didn't have it.

That said, I don't remember feeling bitterness towards him. I never felt like I had to prove anything to his ghost. The first time I met him, I was eighteen. I spent a summer working with him, and was forced to realize how much of my life had unfolded without any male figure to lean on. No one ever stepped into that role.

And yet, I don't hold resentment. In fact, I found forgiveness. My father didn't give me the lessons I wanted, but he gave me something else: the freedom not to have to undo bad lessons. Absent his example, I had the freedom to become whatever kind of man I wanted to. So I've tried to grow into the kind of man who leads with compassion, who fathers with presence, and who understands just how much it matters when your children look up at you with trust in their eyes.

That's how I learned to let go and forgive my father for his absence from my life. Forgiveness, after all, isn't really for the person who wronged you, it's for yourself. Holding onto bitterness only chains you to the past. Forgiving lets you move forward with strength and clarity. My father's absence shaped me, but so did my choice to forgive him. And here's the thing: it's possible that if he was in my life, I would not have been as committed as I am to making my own marriage and family my ultimate priority.

Taking a look at your life is really about shaping your perspective around it. And when you can do that, you can take control of your own destiny. Life is not about a single defining moment. It's about how you choose to meet the moments you're given—the pain and the joy, the presence and the absence, the love and the loss. It's also about how you let those same moments go. Take on the perspective that you are not bound by what you lack. You can take what you were given, forgive the world for what you weren't, and create something new with what you find.

## Going With Grace

All that brings us back to the power of grace; the simple art of letting go. Grace is kindness and compassion, especially for yourself. It's the moment you stop believing that you are "less than," that you are unworthy, or that someone else's failures define you. When you let go of those beliefs, you create space to move forward.

Grace is also about rhythm. You can fight against the music, or you can surrender to it and learn to dance. Life will throw resistance your way in the form of fear, obstacles, and setbacks. You can strain against them until you exhaust yourself, or you can learn to flow with them, staying in rhythm, letting the energy move through you instead of breaking you.

This doesn't mean ignoring the hard things. It means recognizing that the same rhythm that carries the lows also carries the highs. You dance with both. You roll with both. You trust that the music will change, and you'll still be standing.

Grace, forgiveness, and perspective don't exist in a vacuum. They're all part of the same practice. Together they help you find the strength to let go of what holds you back, and the faith you need to keep moving forward.

# ABOUT THE AUTHOR

Sean Martin is a devoted husband, father of two, and serial entrepreneur who rebuilt his life from the ground up after incarceration.

What began as dreams scribbled in a prison notebook became the blueprint for multiple seven- and eight-figure businesses. Now a transformational speaker, coach and commercial real estate investor, Sean mentors entrepreneurs and shows others how to turn struggle into strategy, and purpose into power.